SUPPLY CHAIN
IN NINETY MINUTES

For a complete list of Management Books 2000 titles,
visit our website on www.mb2000.com

The original idea for the 'In Ninety Minutes' series was
presented to the publishers by Graham Willmott, author
of 'Forget Debt in Ninety Minutes'. Thanks are due to
him for suggesting what has become a major series to
help business people, entrepreneurs, managers,
supervisors and others to greatly improve their personal
performance, after just a short period of study.

Proposed titles in the 'in Ninety Minutes' series are:

Forget Debt in Ninety Minutes
Understand Accounts in Ninety Minutes
Working Together in Ninety Minutes
Supply Chain in Ninety Minutes
Networking in Ninety Minutes
25 Management Techniques in Ninety Minutes
Practical Negotiating in Ninety Minutes
Find That Job in Ninety Minutes
Control Credit in Ninety Minutes
Faster Promotions in Ninety Minutes
Managing Your Boss in Ninety Minutes
Better Budgeting in Ninety Minutes
... other titles may be added

The series editor is James Alexander

Submissions of possible titles for this series or for management books in
general will be welcome. MB2000 are always keen to discuss possible new
works that might be added to their extensive list of books for people who
mean business.

SUPPLY CHAIN
in 90 Minutes

Stuart Emmett

2000

First published in 2005 by Management Books 2000 Ltd
Forge House, Limes Road
Kemble, Cirencester
Gloucestershire, GL7 6AD, UK
Tel: 0044 (0) 1285 771441/2
Fax: 0044 (0) 1285 771055
E-mail: info@mb2000.com
Web: www.mb2000.com

Printed and bound in Great Britain by 4edge Ltd of Hockley, Essex - www.4edge.co.uk

British Library Cataloguing in Publication Data is available

ISBN 1-85252-476-6

Contents

About the book and the author   **7**

1 Introduction   **9**
What is the supply chain?   9
  ● *Supply chain Rules 1 and 2*   *14*
Supply chain history   15
Supply chain growth   16
The value chain   19
The benefits of a supply chain management approach   20
  ● *Supply chain rule 3*   *23*

2 Five Key Aspects for a Supply Chain Management   **24**
  1   Lead Time   25
  ● *Supply chain rule 4*   *29*
  2   Customer service   30
  ● *Supply chain rule 5*   *33*
  3   Adding Value   33
  ● *Supply chain rule 6*   *35*
  4   Trade offs   36
  ● *Supply chain rule 7*   *36*
  5   Information   37
  ● *Supply chain rule 8*   *40*

3 Supply Chain Management Changes Traditional Ways   **41**
From traditional ways to new ways   41
From interfacing to integrating   41
Doing something or doing nothing options   43
Demand amplifications   43
Transactional or collaboration approaches   45
Contrasting the Type I and Type II supply chain   48

4 Supply Chain Operations   **52**
    Purchasing/'Buy'   52
    Production/'Make'   59
    Physical Distribution/'Move'   64
    Marketing/'Sell'   67

5 Supply chain Strategy   **71**
    Mission-vision   71
    Inventory   72
    Supply chain KPIs   99
    Supply chain metrics and strategies   102
    Supply chain analysis   103
    Supply chain trends   104

6 Supply chain thinking and approaches   **106**
    Quality Management   106
    Reverse logistics   108
    Collaborative supply chains   109
    Supply Chain re-thinking   113
    The 10 signs of World class supply chain management   124

About this Book and the Author

The development of the supply chain has moved on at a fast pace since the late 1980s and many excellent texts do now exist on detailed aspects of the discipline/philosophy.

However, there is still not anything that gives a concise overview; hence this book has been written.

In writing this book, I have made best-efforts endeavours not to include anything that if used, would be injurious or cause financial loss to the user. However, users are strongly recommended before applying or using any of the contents, to check and verify their own company policy/requirements. No liability will be accepted by the author for the use of any of the contents.

Throughout this book, I have used many 'compare and contrast' and 'ideal-typical' tables.

These are there to give a polarised 'extremes' view. This can however make comparisons appear as being purely being black and white. I do accept fully that such stereotyping is rarely going to be 100% representative of the complex reality found in real life situations; here reality will so often be found 'blurred in the grey zones' between such black/white stereotyping.

It is however, a very valid and a most useful methodology to focus onto the differences. This then means that readers are able to reflect and theorise, before making practical pragmatic decisions that will fit their own reality and circumstances.

Because of the integrative nature of supply chain management, it is somewhat difficult to place items in certain chapters. The contents therefore do have some degree of overlap between them. The inventory topic for example is a difficult one to place, as it is so central to Supply Chain management. I finally decided to put it in the section on Strategy and as this section is towards the end of the book, I hope that those who read sequentially will be then better able to place the central important and integrative aspects of inventory, after reading the earlier parts of the book.

My own journey to 'today' whilst an individual one, does not happen, thankfully without other people's involvement. I smile when I remember so many helpful people. It can also happen in a lifetime of learning and meeting people, that the original source of an idea or information has been forgotten. If I have actually omitted in this book to give anyone the credit they are due, I apologise and hope they will contact me so I can correct the omission in future editions.

So to anyone who has ever had contact with me – then please be assured you will have contributed to my own learning, growing and developing. If you ask me how, then I will tell you – I promise! Whilst thanking you all, my hope is that I have given something positive back to you.

After over 30 years doing a 'proper' job in industry, I decided to become a freelance independent mentor/coach, trainer and consultant trading under the name of Learn and Change Limited. I now enjoy working all over the UK and also on four other continents, principally in Africa and the Middle East, but also in the Far East and South America. Additional to undertaking training, I also am involved with one-to-one coaching/mentoring, consulting, writing, assessing and examining for professional institutes' qualifications and as an external examiner for an MSc in Purchasing and Logistics.

I can be contacted at **stuart@learnandchange.com** or by visiting **www.learnandchange.com**

Introduction

What is the Supply Chain?

The term *Supply Chain* is the process, which integrates, coordinates and controls the movement of goods, materials and information from a supplier to a customer to the final consumer.

The essential point with a supply chain is that it links all the activities between suppliers and customers to the consumer in a timely manner. Supply chains therefore involve the activities of buying/sourcing, making, moving, and selling. The supply chain 'takes care of business' following from the initial customer/consumer demand. Nothing happens with supply until there is an order; it is the order that drives the whole process.

Indeed, some people logically argue that the term supply chain could be called the demand chain.

So the Supply Chain bridges the gap between the fundamental core business aspects of Supply & Demand, as shown below:

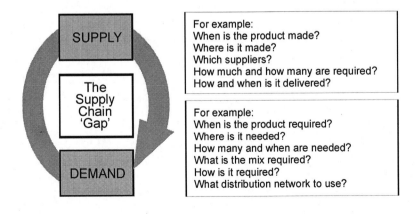

SUPPLY

The Supply Chain 'Gap'

DEMAND

For example:
When is the product made?
Where is it made?
Which suppliers?
How much and how many are required?
How and when is it delivered?

For example:
When is the product required?
Where is it needed?
How many and when are needed?
What is the mix required?
How is it required?
What distribution network to use?

The philosophy of Supply Chain Management is to view all these processes as being related holistically so that they:

- integrate, co-ordinate and control ...
- the movement of materials, inventory and information ...
- from suppliers through a company to meet all the customer(s) and the ultimate ...
- consumer requirements ...
- in a timely manner.

A diagrammatic view follows, where it will be seen that the flows of products and the flows of information are represented by ideas, order creation, and cash/orders:

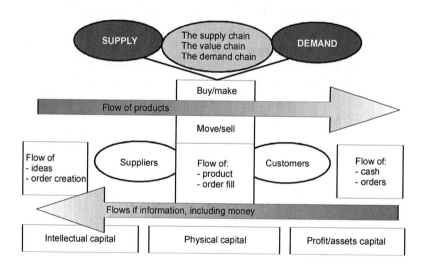

In the above diagram:
- the demand chain represents the creation of demand, for example, marketing and selling with product development
- the supply chain represents fulfilment, for example, procurement and buying, production and making with distribution and moving

- the value chain represents performance, for example, financial measures and capital.

The activities of Buying-Making-Moving and Selling take place in the operational functions of Purchasing, Production, Distribution and Marketing. If each of these functions were to work independently, then inventory stock levels will increase not only internally, but also across the supply chains that feed in and out from a company.

It is also important to realise that each company has not one supply chain, but many, as it deals with different suppliers and has different customers. For each individual finished product or line item, whilst some of the buying, making, moving and selling processes will be identical or very similar, the total supply chain for each product will be different and will involve often a complex network. This also goes, for example, far beyond the first supplier and includes the supplier's supplier, then that supplier's supplier and so on.

Many companies in their supply chain management do not work on the supply chain in this way and often stop with the first level supplier; they seem to forget that the supply chain is effectively a large network of supplier/customer players.

Additionally, different types of business and industry sectors will have different views of what the supply chain is about for them, for example:

- retailers are driven by customer demand creation and the availability/fulfilment of a variety of products
- oil companies are driven by production, so supporting production by the supply side is of more importance
- car assemblers are more consumer demand driven, meaning closer integration of the supply and demand sides.

Different business may be classified to show the influences of their operating environments with the key driver highlighted:

	High complexity	Low complexity
High uncertainty	Capital intensive industries Aerospace Shipbuilding Construction Fitness for purpose (of product)	Fast moving consumer goods Cosmetics Textiles Food and drink Time to market
Low uncertainty	Consumer goods Automotive White goods Electrical goods Value for money	Staple primary industries: Paper Glass Simple components Price (from production productivity

As supply chains differ, then multiple supply chain management is perhaps a better description but it is a cumbersome one. At a simple level, consider the following supply chain (part only) for Lee Cooper jeans:

Customers: World wide via agents, wholesalers and retailers, from the factory in Tunisia that gets supplies of:

- denim cloth from Italy, who use dye from West Germany and cotton from Benin, West Africa and Pakistan
- zips from West Germany, who use wire for the teeth from Japan and polyester tape from France
- thread from Northern Ireland, who use dye from Spain and fibre from Japan
- rivets and Buttons from USA , who use zinc from Australia and copper from Namibia
- pumice (used in stonewashing) from Turkey.

With supply chain management therefore, there are many different supply chains to manage. These supply chain networks will contain companies from all the main following sectors:

- **Primary sector**: Raw materials from farming/fishing (food, beverages and forestry), quarrying/mining (minerals, coals, metals) or drilling (oil, gas, water).

- **Secondary sector**: Conversion of raw materials into products; milling, smelting, extracting, refining into oils/chemicals/ products and then maybe machining, fabricating, moulding, assembly, mixing, processing, constructing into components, sub -assemblies, building construction, structures and furniture, electronic, food, paper, metal, chemicals and plastic products.

- **Service or tertiary sector**: business, personal and entertainment services which involve the channels of distribution from suppliers to customers, via direct, wholesale or retail channels. Services include packaging, physical distribution, hotels, catering, banking, insurance, finance, education, public sector, post, telecoms, retail, repairs etc.

Companies will therefore have many supply chains both internally and externally that interact through a series of simple to complex networks.

Start at 'home'
The starting point however, must be to firstly examine the internal supply chain. Too many companies start into Supply Chain Management, (with much time and effort), by working 'only' with the closest suppliers and customers. They should however first ensure that all their internal operations and activities are 'integrated, co-ordinated and controlled.' Companies may usefully ask their suppliers and customers, if their internal supply chain is working well; they may be surprised by the answer.

Therefore: **Supply Chain Rule Number One** is:

Supply Chain Rule Number One

'Win the home games first.'

Manage the inventory

In the supply chain then, the flows of goods and information will need coordinating to minimise inventory levels. Levels of inventory that are too high can be viewed as the main 'poorly' symptom of a supply chain and the root cause needs 'treatment'. Additionally and as noted above, in supply chain management, there are many different supply chains to manage and these supply chains will usually contain companies in many different sectors; all of these companies in the network can have 'poorly' inventory.

As has been said, holding stock is an admission of defeat in supply chain management. Stock holding is anti-flow and can be analogous to water flowing. Water does not always flow evenly and at the same pace everywhere along a stream. Water sometimes gets trapped in deep pools, is blocked by rocks and other obstacles hidden below the surface. These rock and obstacles impede the smooth, swift flow of the stream. Here the stream represents the flow of goods and information in the supply chain. The pools of water are the inventory holdings and the rocks/obstacles represent the waste in the process from poor quality, re-order, returned goods etc. If a stream is to flow fast and clear, then the rocks and obstacles have to be removed. To do this, the water (and inventory) level has to be lowered so that the rocks are exposed.

Inventory can therefore be hiding more fundamental problems that are currently being hidden from view, and as such, inventory can be seen as the 'root of all evil' in the supply chain. Inventory is therefore the common component throughout the total Supply Chain where it is held either as raw material, sub assemblies/work in progress or as finished goods (which are often held at multiple places in the supply chain).

This gives us **Rule Number Two**.

Supply Chain Rule Number Two

'The format of inventory and where it is held is of common interest to all supply chain players and must be to be jointly investigated and examined.'

Supply chain history

In the UK, the history of the supply chain can be viewed as passing through three phases. However, with any such stereotyping, there is much overlap but at least an 'ideal-typical' view is provided that enables key areas to be viewed more clearly.

Attribute	Functional Supply Chains to the 1980s	Responsive Supply Chains in the 1990s	Adaptive Supply Chains in the 2000s
Integration focus	Over the wall Reactive/quick fixes Monopoly suppliers	Transactional Responsive Competition in suppliers	Collaboration Decision/ proactive Joined up networks of enterprises

Customer focus	Customer can wait 'You will get it when we can send it.'	Customer wants it soon 'You will have it when you want it.'	Customer wants it now 'You will get it.'
Organisation focus	Departmental and ring fencing	Intra-enterprise 'internal' involvement	Extended enterprise involvement
Product positioning	Make to stock Decentralised stock holding Store then deliver	Assemble to order Centralised stock holding Collect and cross dock	Make to order Minimal stock holding Whatever is needed
Management approach	Hierarchical	Command and control	Collaborative
Technology focus	Point solution	ERP	Web connected
Time focus for the business	Weeks to months	Days to weeks	Real time
Performance focus	Cost	Cost and service	Revenue and profits
Collaboration	Low	Medium	High level
Response times	Static	Medium	Dynamic

Supply chain growth

Supply chains have grown like the UK road system. Roads developed over time from basic tracks between local supply and demand centres and they tended to be built in line with the environment, for example, around hills and down valleys, taking an indirect route. The contrast with the more recent motorway networks now allows for more direct movements and a holistically designed network that also separates out fast and slow movers. The developments in roads and in supply chain management have therefore been similar:

- simple to complex
- indirect to direct
- mixed to separated flows
- slow to fast movement.

As supply chains have grown and developed, there have been many words used to describe supply chain management, and the following can be observed. Again, the following stages do 'blur' and they are not mutually exclusive.

Main concentration and aim	Names used and time period	Flow type and the main parts involved
Sheds/trucks	Warehousing and transport are 'separated' 1950s	Physical flows 'Move'
Physical networks and inventory reduction	Physical distribution management (PDM) 1960s	Physical flows
Centralised inventory	Material management + PDM 1970s	Physical flows 'Buy-make-move'
Eliminate inventory	Logistics management 1980s	Physical + information 'Buy-make-move'
Continuous replenishment	Supply chain management 1990s	Physical + information 'Buy-make-move'
Zero lead time and total visibility	Demand pipeline management 2000s	Physical + information 'Buy-make-move'

Whether the phrase **demand pipeline management** will become common, remains to be seem. However it does reflect that the supply is 'kick started' by demand and that without demand, there is no supply chain. Additionally, a pipeline analogy can be used as one of the main aims for Supply Chain Management – for smooth flows of goods and information that are instantly available 'on tap' from a pipe. This analogy however should not be taken to suggest that the supply chain represents a linear and seamless fixed pipe with a stable, controllable, and self-propelling flow, which is sealed from outside influences. Supply chains are rarely like this and, for example, external influences can disrupt plans and expectations for the supply chain. Additionally as will be seen later, linear supply chain thinking can be very limiting and restrictive.

Concurrent with the above changes and developments, have also been changes to general business approaches and technology. The following table shows these changes.

	'Steady as we go' approaches	'Let's go, get ready' approaches
Business	Individual business process making	Collaborative integrated approaches
	Fixed organisational structures	Dynamic and changing flexible structures
	Steady and slow economic growth	Unpredictable growth
	Long product life cycles	'Fashion' and shorter product life cycles
	Passive at best, reactive	Proactive management
	Fixed costs	Variable costs
Technology	Standard IT systems	Open integrated systems
	Labour intensive	Automated and self-managed
	Users adapt to technology	Technology adapts to users

The value chain

Some observers have the view of the supply chain representing a value chain. Michael Porter of Harvard Business School in his book 'Gaining Competitive Advantage' introduced this concept in 1985. From the diagram below (reproduced with permission from Cheltenham Tutorial College), you will see this has large implications for the supply chain.

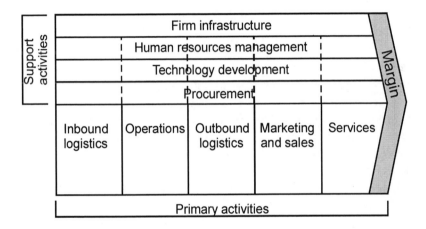

This divides into primary and support activities as follows:

Primary activities

- **Inbound logistics** covering stores, warehousing, handling and stock control
- **Operations** covering production and packing and all activities that transfer inputs into outputs
- **Outbound logistics** include transport and warehouse networks to get products to customers
- **Marketing and sales** cover the methods by which customers know about and purchase products
- **Services** includes the support for all activities such as installation, returns.

Support activities

- **Procurement** includes the buying and purchasing of products as well as all other resources
- **Technology** covers things information and communications technology (ICT) and research and development (R&D)
- **Human resource management** covers all aspects concerned with personnel
- **Infrastructure** covers finance, legal and other general management activities.

Porter then expanded this concept of a Value Chain into a Value System. This consists of a series of linked value chains. By this joining together of value chains into a value system, in effect we create a supply chain. Where the value actually is, according to Porter, is dependant on the way that a customer uses the product and not just totally on the costs incurred through buying, making and moving it. These costs include all the raw materials and activities that create the product, which then represent its value. But after this, it is only when the product is purchased that the value can be measured; and finally, it is not until the product is at the final customer/consumer that the real value is to be found.

Part of the difficulty here is that each individual organisation in the supply chain will attempt to define value themselves by looking at its own profitability. Each company will in turn carry on this definition to their suppliers and as the value definition moves back up the chain, then it will become distorted. Indeed, another reason for companies to try to work together more closely with suppliers and customers is to have a constant view of value throughout the supply/value chain.

The benefits of a Supply Chain Management approach

The real competition in business comes not just from companies competing against each other, but increasingly comes from competing supply chains where there is an approach to maximise benefits from the supply chain beyond first level suppliers.

Competitive advantage is to found by doing things better or by doing thing cheaper.

Looking for these advantages extends from within a company, towards the supply chains. This will mean looking to remove sub-functional conflicts from all the interdependent processes, whether these processes are internal or external to a business. Accordingly, it is the supply chain that now provides the competitive advantage for a business. This will in turn mean taking a collaborative supply chain approach to examine and to total the costs of all the functions, matched to the service levels. If this is not done, and by continuing to minimise the costs for each sub function, then this could mean:

- buying in bulk from multiple sources, (Purchasing is only being optimised); but for example, this will give high storage costs
- making few products with long production runs, (here Production is only being optimised); which means limited ranges, poor availability etc
- moving in bulk, (Transport only being optimised); but gives infrequent delivery etc.
- selling what produced, (Marketing only being optimised); but it may not be needed.

The way the supply chain is structured and managed is therefore critical and some reported benefits of following a supply chain approach follow. It will be noted that different approaches give different results.

	No supply chain: functional silos	Internal integrated supply chain	Plus, external integration to the first level only
Inventory days of supply Indexed	100	78	62
Inventory carrying cost % sales	3.2%	2.1%	1.5%
On time in Full deliveries	80%	91%	95%
Profit % Sales	8%	11%	14%

It will be seen that with a supply chain approach, inventory costs fall, profit and the service fulfillment increase, and the 'best of both worlds' is achieved for the company undertaking the approach.

Additional benefits of supply chain management will only come when there is an examination of all costs/service levels together with all the players, so as to obtain reduced lead times and improved total costs/service for all parties in the network. This means therefore, going beyond the first tier of suppliers and looking also at the supplier's supplier and so on. It represents more than data and process, it includes mutual interest, open relationships and sharing. It may well mean a total Supply Chain Re-thinking is needed – a topic covered in the final chapter of this book.

So **Supply Chain Rule Number Three** is:

Supply Chain Rule Number Three

'The optimum and the 'ideal' cost/service balance will only ever be found by working and collaborating fully with all players in the Supply Chain.'

A key area here is to balance the service aspects with the costs. 30 to 70 per cent of business cost will be in the Supply Chain. Indeed, cost is a common language to anyone in the supply chain. Efficiently and effectively managing the flows of goods and information across the supply chain networks is therefore essential in bringing about the cost/service balance. A big promise and rarely an easy approach but resulting in the perfect ideals of:

- Increased/improved service, reaction times, product availability etc.
- Reduced/improved total cost, total stock levels, time to market etc.

2

Five Key Aspects for Supply Chain Management

One starting place to develop a better understanding is by mapping a supply chain. This will identify the many parts/players/participants that are involved beyond the first level contacts. Process mapping includes different techniques ranging from simple flow charts to value stream maps and beyond. Process mapping can be a complex process and one that may usefully be led by external people. However, even simple approaches are usually very revealing, for example:

1. Determine the company units involved.
2. Agree steps with the people doing the work.
3. Identify the start and end of each process.
4. Go to the next upstream and downstream processes and repeat steps 1-3.
5. Lay out all the step processes in a flow chart.
6. Insert the lead times between and within each process.
7. Carry on, until all up and down stream processes are identified.

This mapping can also be used to ask all the supply chain players what they want, what they buy, their experiences at the pre-order/order and post-order stages; and to use all this information as the basis for improvements.

Meanwhile by having a record of the current processes with the lead times, the next natural step is to critically examine the lead times.

Key aspect 1: Lead time

Lead time is perhaps the critical component in supply chain management. However it is usually viewed incrementally and sub-optimally. Just as time is cash, and cash flow is important to a business, then also important are the associated flows of goods and information that have generated the cash flow in the first place. The cash to cash cycle time (C2C) is at the root of cash flow and reducing the time from buying to the receipt of payment for sales is therefore critical.

What follows is a basic view of lead time covering all the elements involved, first by looking at the eight types of lead time, then continuing with an analysis of the component parts of these eight types

Eight types of lead time

Lead Time	Action	By
Pre-order planning	User	Customer
Procurement	Order placing	Customer to supplier
Supplier	Order despatching	Supplier
Production	Making to order	Supplier
Warehouse	Supplying from stock	Supplier
Transit	Transporting	Supplier
Receivers	Receiving	Customer
Payment	Paying	Customer to supplier

Component parts of lead times

Lead time	Lead Time Stage	Steps, by date
Pre-Order Planning	User Need	Analysing status to determine need to order
	User Requisition	Need to order to date of order requisition

Procurement	Order preparation	Order requisition to order release date
	Order confirmation	Order release to date of confirmation
Supplier * see also the production and warehouse lead times	All the stages here are in the production and warehouse lead times	Confirmation to order despatched date
Production (e.g. made to order)	Order processing	Date of order receipt to date order accepted/confirmed
	Preparation	Order accepted to date manufacture starts
	Manufacture (queue time, set up, machine/ operator time/inspect/ put away times)	Start of manufacture to date it finishes
	Pack/load (to the Warehouse or to Transit LT)	Finished manufacture to date order despatched
Warehouse (e.g. available ex stock)	In stock	Date goods arrived to date of order receipt
	Order Processing	Order receipt to date order is accepted or confirmed
	Picking	Date order accepted to date order is available/ picked
	Pack/Load (to Warehouse or to Transit LT)	Order available to date order despatched
Transit		Date despatched to date order received
Receiving		Date order received to date available for issue/use

Payment	Credit	Date invoice received or of other 'trigger,' to date payment received
	Payment processing	Date payment received to date cash available for use

Supply lead time

The supply lead time (SLT) used in inventory management should not be confused with the above mentioned *supplier* lead time. The supply lead time is actually the total of all the above lead times, excluding the payment lead times. Effectively therefore, the supply lead time is from the pre-order planning lead time (from analysis of the order status/determining the need to order), right through all the above steps and stages to the receiving lead time (date order received to date available for use/issue). It involves many different parties internally in a business, and also externally, including both the supplier and the customer.

Lead time examination

Lead times must be examined using real examples whilst ensuring that all appropriate stages and steps are included. There may also be additional lead times for some players, for example with imports, the customs clearance lead-time. An example below, using chocolate confectionery, shows some abbreviated results found on lead times.

- **Supply lead time** *(cocoa)*: 180 days on average (once per year crop) with a company in stock lead time of 70 days, (traders are also holding some external stocks)
- **Supply lead time** *(ingredients)*: for example, with nuts 80 days on average (range 10- 120 days) and the in stock of 80 days maximum
- **Supply lead time** *(sugar)*: 1-2 days with in stock lead time of 2 days

- **Supply lead time** *(packaging)*: 1-3 days with in stock lead time of 3 days maximum
- **Production lead time**: 1-2 days but product line batch scheduling can mean waiting for 30 days before the next production run
- **Warehouse & transit lead times** *(distribution)*: 1-5 days with in stock lead time of 30 days minimum to cover for the production lead time.

After each lead time stage has been quantified, analysis will show if there is a way to do things better. It can be expected that reductions in lead times will come from information flows and not the goods flows.

Lead time variability

A crucial aspect when examining lead time is variability as when lead times are realistically looked at, then a range of times will be found; for example from 2 to 8 days. This range represents the variability of lead time and average calculations are of little practical assistance and can be dangerous if used for planning and decision making. It is this variability that so often represents the uncertainty found in the Supply Chain and which was traditionally dealt with by holding safety stocks to cover against such uncertainty.

The variability must however be examined by all those involved, before finally working together to agree that lead times becomes a fixed item. Then the variability and the uncertainty are removed by having fixed known reliable lead times; the length of the lead time being of secondary importance.

The problem of lead variability can be illustrated as follows.

If lead time (LT) is halved from 12 to 6 weeks and lead time variability (LTV) stays the same at + 4 weeks, then:

Current LT			New LT		
LTV	LT	LTV	LTV	LT	LTV
-4	12	+ 4	-4	6	+4
Total LT					
8 to 16 weeks			2 to 10 weeks		

So, if LTV stays the same, then there is higher disruption/costs and reduced speed (index of 1 to 2 from 1 to 5)

The following are some ways to consider in reducing lead time variability.

Demand LTV
- Predictable known orders/ size/ make up
- Predictable order times
- Data accuracy on what customers want/ when/ price
- Is it 'end' demand or is 'institutionalised' through inefficient 'not talking' supply chain players (internal and or external)

Supply LTV
- Predictable known LT
- Get correct quantity first time
- Get correct quality first time
- Data accuracy on what is supplied/ price.

'Uncertainty is the mother of Inventory' as the *length* of lead time is of secondary importance to the *variability* in the lead time.

This gives us **Supply Chain Rule Number Four**.

Supply Chain Rule Number Four

'Time is cash, cash flow is critical and so are the goods and information flows; fixed reliable lead times are more important than the length of the lead time.'

Key aspect 2: Customer service

This is commonly measured by the following:

- **Cycle Lead Time**: e.g. daily delivery service, order day 1 for day 2 delivery
- **Stock Availability**: e.g. 95% orders met from stock
- **Consistency/reliability**: e.g. 95% orders are delivered within 3 days

Actual achievement varies, so the following may be helpful for comparison purposes.

Key performance indicators – average figures from UK manufacturers

(Source: Best Factory Awards 2001)

Industry sector	On time delivery reliability	In full ex stock availability	Stock-turns per annum
Process	91.0%	97.5%	14
Engineering	92.0%	96.0%	13
Electrical	96.0%	98.2%	9
Consumer household	98.1%	99.0%	21

(These stock turns figures can be misleading. These are calculated from financial annual accounts by dividing the sales turnover by the value of the stock assets on hand to give an average yearly figure of stock turn. This would not be the same as the physical stock turns).

Customer importance

It is only the order from the customer that triggers all the activity in the supply chain. Without a customer order, then no supply chain activity is required as the customer is only interested in buying delivered products.

Customer service levels are a variable and each customer service variable has a cost associated with it. The relationship between cost and service is rarely a linear straight line, but more of an exponential curve. So, a ten per cent increase in service may mean for example, cost increase of 15 or over 50 per cent. For example, in transport we pay more for first class mail than for second class mail; we pay more for a service offering an overnight parcel delivery than for a three-day or a deferred delivery.

Customer value

Customers will place a value on many aspects of the total service offering. Value is placed by customers primarily against delivery/ availability and also against quality, the cycle lead-time and the cost and the service levels. As perception is reality, customers can see these as being inter-related or may view them independently. It is therefore important for a business to understand the specific reality as seen by the customer. The following are aspects of the criteria that customers value.

Quality is 'performing right first time every time' and involves:
- meeting requirements
- fitness for purpose
- minimum variance
- elimination of waste
- a continuous improvement culture.

Service, is about 'continually meeting customer needs as the market changes', and involves:
- the support available
- product availability
- flexibility
- reliability
- consistency.

Cost, is about knowing what the costs really are and then looking at how to reduce them. This involves:

- design of product
- manufacturing process
- distribution process
- administration process
- stock levels.

Cycle lead-time is about knowing what the lead times really are and then looking for ways to reduce them. This involves considering:
- time to market
- time from order placement to time available for issue
- response to market forces.

Quality, cost, service and time are all inter-linked and customer value can therefore be seen as:

$$\frac{\text{Increasing (Quality * Service)}}{\text{Reducing (Cost * Lead time)}}$$

A business therefore, ideally will try to improve the quality and the service, whilst, reducing the cost and lead times. All of the aspects are inter-related and connected and for example, it matters not to the majority of customers where the goods come from or whether the goods are transported by road, rail, sea, air etc.

The customer is the reason for the business – so, continually working to serve the customer better is critical. The customer is the business, after all. But who *is* the customer? The traditional view is perhaps the one that pays the invoices, but by seeing the next person/process/operation in the chain as the customer, then this way of thinking means there may well be hundreds of supplier/customer relationships in a single supply chain. If all these 'single' relationships were being viewed as supplier/customer ones, then the 'whole' would be very different.

So we have the next **Supply Chain Rule**.

Supply Chain Rule Number Five

'The Customer is the business; it is the customer's demand that drives the whole supply chain; finding out what customers value and then delivering it, is critical.'

 Key aspect 3: Adding value

This has become common language in business, but seems to be often confused in meaning. For me, there are two different views:

1   **Value is found when something – satisfies a need – conforms to expectations – gives 'pride of ownership', i.e. it is 'valued' over something that is not.**

    Here then the perceptions of value will differ. For example, customers have different perceptions of 'worth' and 'price' – different customers have different perceptions of quality/lead time and the cost/service balance. Maybe therefore, value can be seen as the balance and the pivot point between worth and price or between quality/lead time and cost/service?

2   **Value is the opposite to cost and in most processes, more time is actually spent on adding cost and not on adding value.**

    For example:

    (a) in *manufacturing*, 85% of time = queuing/setting up/ inspecting/storing and handling = cost adding, and 15% of the time = processing/QA = value adding.

    (b) in *warehousing*, 30 days in storage (cost adding), yet only 1 day to pick/pack/load/transit to the customer (value adding).

A business will not find it worthwhile to invest and automate wasteful non-value added activities. Waste is the symptom rather than the root cause of the problem so the aim has to be to investigate the cause and then remove the wasteful non-value adders: those processes that take time and resources without adding any value. Attention should therefore be given to those activities that do add 'real' value, for example: –

- Make it faster through form changes
- Move it faster through time changes
- Get paid faster through place changes.

Adding value in supply chains

Examples are as follows.

From	To
Forecasting	Make to order
Inventory push and stock holding	Inventory pull from order placing
Storing	Sorting
Handling	Postponement
Manual ordering	Automated ordering

A supply chain view of added value would recognise that it is only the movement to the customer that is adding (the ultimate) value. Stopping or delaying the flow adds costs.

Cost and value adders in the supply chain

(Reproduced with permission from Cheltenham Tutorial College)

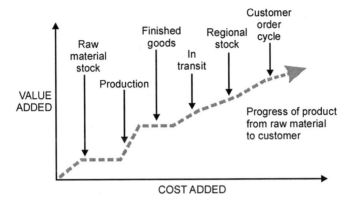

Clearly, this diagram shows that goods being stored are incurring cost and are not adding value. Whilst this will generally be the case, if those goods being stored were appreciating in value, then this would not apply. This would however only apply for a very limited range of products, such as with bullion in non-inflation times and with works of art. The diagram emphasises that movement to the customer as quickly as possible whilst accounting for associated cost levels, is what really counts in adding value. Therefore we have the next **Supply Chain Rule**.

Supply Chain Rule Number Six

'It is only the movement to the customer that adds the ultimate value; smooth continuous flow movements are preferable.'

Key aspect 4: Trade-offs

This involves looking more totally and holistically with all players across the supply chain(s) and examining the total cost/service balance.

Trade-offs are possible in three basic ways:

- **Within functions**, e.g.   cost v product quality
  cost v product availability.

- **Between functions**, e.g.   price v total acquisition cost
  stock v JIT supply.

- **Between companies**, e.g.   transactional v collaborative supply
  dependable v ad hoc supply.

There are therefore many possibilities and opportunities available to integrate/co-ordinate/control across the supply chain(s) networks, starting by 'winning the home games first' in and between the internal functions, followed by all external connections to the supply chain networks.

Here then is **Supply Chain Rule Number Seven**.

Supply Chain Rule Number Seven

'Trade Off by looking holistically with all the supply chain players.'

Key aspect 5: Information requirements within the supply chain

Information is required for every stage of the supply chain and for all levels of supply chain planning.

Advances in both operating systems and computing power make it easier and more economical to obtain this information. Information and communication technology (ICT) enables the collection, analysis and evaluation of data and the transfer of information from one point to another. It attempts to maximise coherent messages and minimise the coupling problems between players. All parts of the supply chain rely on ICT in the planning, operational, administrative and management processes. The customer interface can now be replaced by electronic means. Information can be used and transferred by techniques such as demand forecasting, MRP, JIT and ERP which rely on the electronic gathering and manipulation of data.

Electronic communication enables:
- automatic generation of performance monitoring against pre-set key performance indicators
- automatic tracking of vehicles and loads using global positioning satellites giving constant visibility, improved safety, security and responsive routing and scheduling
- automatic decision making, e.g. stock reordering against pre-set levels and quantities
- proposed changes to networks to be modelled so that the effects can be assessed and decisions made.

Electronic Data Interchange
EDI is the transfer of data from one computer to another by electronic means, using agreed standards. Five main types of data are transferred:
- trade data, e.g. quotation, purchase order
- technical data, e.g. product specifications
- query response e.g. order progressing

- monetary data, e.g. electronic payment of invoice, electronic ticketing
- consignment details, e.g. manifests and customs details.

The use of EDI in the supply chain enables a buyer to have a direct closed network link with a number of its suppliers throughout the supply chain normally referred to as a 'hub'. EDI contributes to shorter lead times and lower stocks. EDI also enables load manifests (people and goods) and Customs data to be transmitted ahead of the shipment, reducing delays in clearing through the import/export process.

Enterprise Resource Planning (ERP)
An ERP system automates the tasks of the major functional areas of an organisation,(finance, HR, sales, production, purchasing and distribution) and stores all the data from those different areas in a single database, accessible by all.

Automatic Planning & Scheduling
APS is generally a module of an ERP or MRP system, which gathers and analyses data on sales, purchases, production and inventory to ensure that the right materials required for the production process are always available at the right time.

Warehouse management systems
WMS provides electronic information concurrent with goods movement and integrates physical operations with ERP systems. WMS allows handling of higher volumes and eases the transition from fixed to random storage for warehouses with fixed location storage.

Automatic identification of inventory
This is a feature of inventory management systems allowing the stock control through devices such as bar coding and RFID – Radio Frequency Identification.

Computer control
Computer controlled systems for storage and MHE, are used in storage systems (e.g. conveyors) and remote controlled MHE.

Computerised routing and scheduling

Routing of transport services can be calculated automatically according to shortest route, quickest route, or any variables chosen. Multi-drop operations can be scheduled to give the optimum sequence of pick-ups and drops according to the information provided.

Modelling

Planners use computer programs to predict flows through new and modified networks and to assess proposals in terms of cost and benefit.

E-business

Electronic business refers generally to commercial transactions that are based upon the processing and transmission of digitised data, including text, sound and visual images and that are carried out over open networks (like the Internet) or closed networks that have a gateway onto an open network (Extranet).

E-business is a form of EDI but it uses open, as opposed to closed, networks – some of the E-business applications are as follows:

- Business to Business Trading Exchanges provide a two way on-line link between buyers and suppliers; they are now often referred to as a 'marketplace'. Suppliers can advertise their products and services through electronic catalogues; buyers can order from supplier catalogues, take part in auctions, or conduct tendering online; buyers can book travel. In industries with large numbers of buyers and suppliers, third parties generally organise and manage online forums. In industries with few buyers and a large number of sellers, the buyers often own and run the markets.

- Individual consumers and any system user can get up to-the-minute information, make enquiries, place orders and payments can be made on-line. Information about the current position and status of orders services can also be obtained. Some E-business examples follow:

Supply Chain aspect	Buying	Ordering	Designing products	Post sales
Information	Sharing with suppliers	Visibility	Sharing with suppliers	Customer use use records
Planning	Coordinating when to replenish	Forecast sharing/ agreements	New product launching	Service planning
Product flow	Paperless exchanges	Automated	Product changes	Automatic replacement of parts
KPIs	Compliance monitoring	Logistics track and trace	Project monitoring	Performance measurement
Business changes from 'E'	On line auctions, market exchanges	Click on ordering	Mass customis- ation	Remote sensing and diagnostics, download upgrades

Information is required therefore for every stage of the supply chain and for all levels of supply chain planning.

All parts of the supply chain rely on ICT in the planning, operational, administrative and management processes.

This gives us the last of the eight **Supply Chain Rules**.

Supply Chain Rule Number Eight

'Information flows lubricate the supply chain; using appropriate ICT is critical.'

3

Supply Chain Management Changes Traditional Ways

Many supply chains will need to change so they can fully benefit from taking a supply chain management approach. It is useful therefore to have some brief overviews of what may need to change.

From traditional ways to new ways

From traditional ways ⟶ To new ways

From traditional ways	To new ways
Independence	**Integration**
Independent of next link	Dependency
Links are protective	End/end visibility
Means uncertainty	More certainty
Unresponsive to change	Quicker response
High cost, low service	High serve, lower cost
Fragmented internally	'Joined up' structures
Blame culture	'Gain' culture
Competing companies	Competing supply chains

From interfacing to integrating

The supplier/customer relationship can also change, for example:

From interfacing ◄───────► **To integrating**

Supplier selection	Supplier collaboration
Arms length	Total commitment
Confrontation and power based	Cooperation/collaboration
Day to day short term	Year to year and beyond
Clear cut ordering	EDI/Visibility
Transactional	Partnership/collaboration
Separated culture	Aligned cultures
Little trust	Extensive trust
Inspect and penalise	Quality assured

In turn this may mean changes in the following aspects.

Aspect	From	To	Means
Order Lot size	Large Less frequent orders	Small More frequent orders	Reduced order quantities
Suppliers	Multi sourcing Short contract	Single sourcing Long term contracts	Fewer Suppliers Lower costs
	Transactional	No defects	Shared developments
	Rejects Low price	Quality Total Acquisition cost	
	Arm's length	Collaboration	
Scheduling	Suppliers	Buyers	Less variability
Lead Times	Long	Shorter	Less stocks

To summarise the benefits from taking a supply chain management approach, we can find the *doing something* or *doing nothing* options.

Doing something or doing nothing options

What needs to be done	The 'do nothing' option
A few long term suppliers and joint action teams	Adversary, play offs with suppliers
Short production runs with quick changeovers	Long product runs of products no longer needed
Minimal JIT stockholding	'Just in case' expensive stock holding
Customers who are more demanding	Customers who get fed up, so go elsewhere
Right first time quality throughout	Inspections, reworking, warranty claims
Process & flatter cross functional management structures	Vertical, silo management structures
'Empowered', proactive 'fire lighting' managers	'Turf conscious', reactive 'fire fighting' managers
Continuous improvement and change	'Rowing the same boat upstream' and resisting change

Demand amplifications

The need to 'Work Together' has been shown both internally and externally. If this is not done, then *demand can be amplified as it passes down the chain*, (The 'Forrester effect'). In a four player supply chain then, the following will typically occur with the stock levels:

Factory ◄──► Distributor ◄──► Wholesaler ◄──► Retailer
250   245   205   100

Note: these figures represent stock levels, being indexed at 100. So the multiple, for example at the factory end is times 2.5

This increase in stock and the 'bullwhip' effect is explained by the following diagram, where it will be seen that each player is holding safety stock as a protection from both the uncertainty in supply and, or demand.

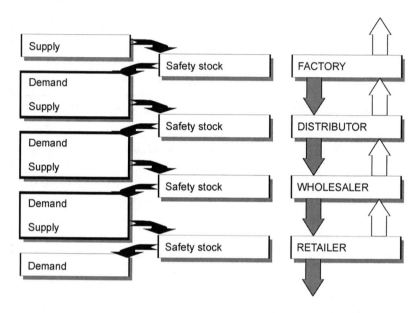

The only way to prevent such realities is by having all the four players integrate, coordinate and control together. For example, if the factory and distributor and wholesaler had visibility of the retailers end demand and were all working collaboratively.

This effect has been shown above in a single supply chain. Imagine the impacts on, the common reality of, multiple level supply chains and networks?

Demand replenishment in networks

The reality for most players in supply chain management is that they have multiple levels of supply chain involvements. Therefore managing inventory in a sequential and simple supply chain is different from that found when having to manage inventory across these multiple level supply chains, for example within a distribution network or across many different players. The following will show some of differences:

Key Area	Simple supply chain	Multiple supply chain
Objective for inventory levels	Incremental view per DC/stock holding place	Total view across the supply chain
Demand forecasts	Independent at each level	Based on end customer
Lead times	Work on first level suppliers' lead time and variability	Use all/holistic lead times
Forrester effects	Ignored, 'not my problem'	Measured and allowed for in replenishment planning
Visibility	To first level supplier and customer only	Holistic visibility
Customer service	Differentiation is not possible	Differentiation is possible
Cost implications	Incremental costs giving high holistic cost levels	Modelled for optimisation across the supply chain

Transactional or collaboration approaches

The required change from transactional/responsive to collaborative/ adaptive supply chains makes an interesting comparison. Another 'ideal-typical' comparison follows.

Transactional	Collaboration
Price/Risk	
Price orientation	Total cost of ownership
Price dominates	Shared destiny dominates
One way	Two way exchanges
Customer demands sensitive data	Exchanges of sensitive data
Customer keeps all cost savings	Mutual efforts to reduce costs, times and waste

All risk with supplier, the buyer risks little	Shared risk and benefits
'What is in it for me?'	'What is in it for us?'
Short term	Long term

Negotiations	
Strong use of ploys in negotiations	Mutual gains 'rule' discussions
Power based	Equality based
Win/lose	Win/win
'One off' deals	'For ever' together
'One night stand'	'Marriage'
Walk in and out of, change is easy.	Difficult to break, change is difficult
Easy to set up	Difficult to set up
Adversarial and maybe inefficient for one party	Challenging to implement and continue with
'Partnershaft'	Partnership

Inter-personal relationships	
No personal relationships	Strong personal relationship
Separated/arms length	Close/alliance
Low contact/closed	Shared vision/open
Predatory power based	Proactive and more people based
Hierarchical /superior subordinate	Equality
Blame culture	Problem solving 'gain' culture
Alienated employees	Motivated employees

Trust	
Trust is based on what the contract says = contractual trust	Trust is based on goodwill, commitment and cooperation
Little ongoing trust	Continual trust plus risk/benefits sharing
Power based 'spin'	Pragmatic 'tough' trust.

Controls	
Strong on tactical/ departmental controls	Strong on marketing strategy and supply chain alignment

High formal controls	Self controlled
Rigid contracts	Flexible contracts
Technical performance and the specifications 'rule'	Work beyond just 'one' technical view
Resource and capacity capabilities	Mutual long term capabilities
Measure by non compliance	Both measure and agree remedial action

The change from transactional methods to collaborative approaches goes far beyond the technical issues of, say, ICT connectivity, and fully embraces the soft skills. If only all the supply chain parties would work together, then a lot more would get done more efficiently and more effectively. The evidence for this from relationship principles seems overwhelming yet many will not subscribe to mutually sharing a collaborative supply chain management approach.

A major reason for this is that business is founded on power. For example, the supplier's 'anger at unreasonable demands, unsustainable prices and the rejection of high quality produce' by a supermarket company (Sandra Bell). Therefore two-way collaboration can sit here as an uneasy concept; it is easy to 'beat up' on someone when you have some power over their business/life. Another major reason for the lack of two-way collaborative approaches is also that soft skills are the hard skills for many people in business.

Supply chain management collaboration between companies will not succeed without appropriate recognition that soft skill development is required; after all, any relationship depends on trust - and without trust, there is no relationship. Again very simple to say, yet many do not realise this and if they do, they do not practice it; an important topic we shall return to in the later section on Supply Chain Thinking.

Contrasts between Type I and Type II supply chains

The following model for two types of supply chain presents an 'extremes' view to stimulate debate and discussion about the changes that may be needed. The reality and the practice will be found mainly in the 'grey' between the 'black/white' extremes. Also, some aspects can be mixed between the two types. For example Type I on the main drivers and products; but Type II on inventory and buying etc.

Attribute	Type I Supply Chain **Production led** **Push** **More about supply**	Type II Supply Chain **Market led** **Pull** **More about demand**
Main driver	Forecast driven Growth from volume output and ROI. Financial performance profit driven. 'Pump' push From Supply to demand Mass production	Order driven Growth from customer satisfaction Customer focus, value driven 'Turn on the Tap' pull From demand to supply Mass market
Products	Launched Functional, standard, commodities Low variety Long product life cycle	Transition Innovative, design and build, fashion goods High variety Short product life cycles
Inventory	'Turns' Stock holding Just in case Hold safety stock Seen as an asset/ protection	'Spins' Little stock holding Just in time No safety stock Seen as a liability

'Buying'	Buy goods for anticipated and projected demand/needs.	Assign capacity on a daily basis
	Instructed suppliers	Involved suppliers
	Arms length, played off on a short term basis.	Committed suppliers, long term
	Confrontation	Cooperation
	Adversarial	Alliances
	Narrow range of suppliers	Ordered supplier base of specialists
	Low cost buying	Total acquisition cost buying
	Inspection on receipt	Quality assured
'Making'	'Build'	'Supply'
	Proactive to orders	Reactive to orders
	Economy of scale	Reduce waste
	Continuous flow and mass production	Batch, job shop, project methods of production, 'customising'.
	Long runs	Short runs
	Low production costs	Higher production costs
	High work in progress inventory	Low work in progress inventory
	High plant efficiency, e.g. 24/7	High effectiveness but with lower plant efficiencies
	Labour is an extension the machine	Labour brings the continuous of improvements
	Ordered 'push' schedules and reliable demand forecasts/make to stock.	Flexible 'pull' Kanban schedules with make/assemble to order
'Moving'	Move slower in bulk	Move faster in smaller quantities
	Large/less frequent deliveries	Smaller, frequent deliveries
	Storage is high cost	Storage is low cost
	Transport is a low cost	Transport costs are higher
	Fewer but larger RDC type deliveries	Many varied and dispersed destinations

Customers	Predictive demand Cost driven Are only handled at the top or by the 'customer service' department	Un-predictive demand Availability driven Everybody is customer focussed
Information	Demand information is sometimes passed back Used mainly for 'executing'	Demand information is mandatory Used also for planning purposes
Handling of customers' orders	10% forecast error and algorithmetic based forecasts Continuous scheduled replenishment More 'push' Stock outs rarer (1-2%) and are dealt with contractually Stable and consistent orders, some predictable weekly type ordering Clear cut ordering Service levels are more rigid	40-100% error with forecasts more consultative based Real time visibility throughout the supply chain More 'pull' Stock outs are immediate and frequent (10-40% p.a.) and volatile Cyclical demand, many orders, unpredictable orders EDI/Visibility ordering Service levels are more flexible to actual forecasts
Deliver from stock lead times	Immediate, fast in one or two days	Immediate to long; slower and from days to weeks
Make to order lead times	1-6 months as mainly making 'standard' products for stock.	1-14 days
Costs	Mainly in physical conversion/movements Inventory costs in finished goods	Mainly in marketing Inventory costs in raw materials/wip

	Cost control very strong and any gained savings are retained	Revenue generation and any gained savings are shared
Producer selling price	Low selling price Few markdowns 5-20% profits Low risk	Higher selling price Many end of season markdowns 20-60% profits Higher risk levels
Organisation methods	Silo/hierarchical management with some 'cells' 'Top down' to staff gives orders and responsibility Professional managers are more driven by power Transactional/ownership Self interest Protective interfacing links Slow to change, change is mainly resisted, with maintenance of the 'status quo' Internal fragmentation with instructed employees Tendency for 'blame' cultures 'Fire-lighting' Little trust People a liability and numbers are to be reduced wherever possible Narrow skill base Outside recruitment 'Do what you are told'	Flatter structures with cross functional teams Top down and bottom up, giving assistance – everybody is responsible Leaders/educators who are who people driven Partnership/collaborative Customer interest Visible integrated links Quicker response with continuous improvement and more embracive of change 'Joined up' structures with involved employees More 'gain' structure 'Fire-fighting' Extensive trust People are an asset to be invested in Multiple skill bases Internal recruitment also 'Do what you think is best'

4

Supply Chain Operations

Within each component/functional process of the supply chain, (buying, making, moving and selling), specific aspects can be found that will assist in supply chain optimisations. These 'what is done' operations, will be examined in this section.

Purchasing – 'buy'

Before buying any goods or services, fundamental questions to be asked are:

1. Is it needed?
2. Can the need be met in another way?
3. Is it already to be found elsewhere within the company?
4. Can the requirement be met by sharing rather that purchasing?
5. Can the requirement be met by renting rather than by purchasing?
6. Is the quantity required essential?
7. Can it serve any useful purpose after its initial use?
8. Is the value added to the business greater than the total cost of ownership?

The total cost of ownership (TCO)

This is a philosophy that includes **value**. The total cost of ownership sees that the benefit of ownership only comes when the value added to the business through owning the asset, is greater than the TCO.

Conceptually therefore:
TCO = price + total acquisition cost (TAC) + life cycle costs (LCC), or whole life costs (WLC)

Both TAC and WLC are examined below.

Total acquisition cost (TAC)
This is the price paid plus, all the 'other' costs paid by the buyer:

- **quality**, e.g. errors, defects, returns
- **delivery**, e.g. modes, time scales
- **delivery performance**, e.g. non-availability, unreliability
- **lead time**, e.g. stock financing
- **packing**, e.g. point of display repacks
- **warehousing**, e.g. extra handling
- **inventory**, e.g. product deterioration
- **new supplier**, e.g. start-ups, assessments, negotiations
- **administration**, e.g. orders processing.

The 'real' question to ask is what are these 'other' costs?

Whole life costing (WLC)
This is the same as life cycle costing and can be defined as:

The systematic consideration of all relevant costs and revenues associated with the acquisition and ownership of the asset and a means of comparing options and their associated cost and revenue over a period of time.

WLC covers:
- Initial capital/procurement costs, e.g. design, construction, installation, purchase, or leasing fees and charges.
- Future costs, e.g. all operating costs (rent, rates, cleaning, inspection, maintenance, repair, placements/renewals, energy, dismantling, disposal, security, and management).
  Note – unplanned and unexpected maintenance/refurbishment

may amount to more than half of the initial capital spent.
- Opportunity costs, e.g. the cost of not having the money available for alternative investments, which would earn money, or the interest payable on loans to finance work.

Purchasing portfolios

These examine critical aspects to be examined to establish the strategic importance of a product to the business.

1 Risk/spend by products and by relationships

Product categories:

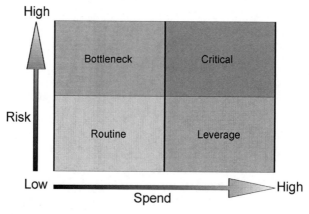

The following examples are taken from the oil/gas and the confectionery manufacturing sectors.

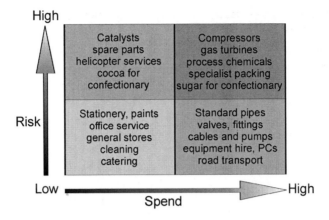

Relationships

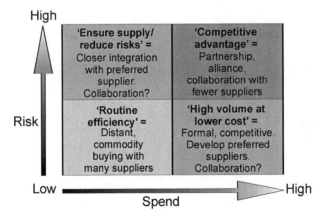

These indicate that different products have different strategic requirements to a business. It also gives a broad indication of how supplier relationships can be conducted into the following four basic strategies:

● **Routine items:** Routine buying of commodities, needing efficiency. Relationships maybe conducted at 'arms length' for those low value items required irregularly.

55

- **Critical items:** Need here is to ensure the supply and reduce the risk

- **Leverage items:** where a high volume is purchased therefore needing to obtain at the lowest cost

- **Bottleneck/strategic items:** requiring competitive advantage. These will involve longer term relationships and partnering approaches with suppliers

2 Suppliers/buyers power

The balance of power in the four above positions on risk will not be 'equal.' This is shown in the following diagram where the variation in approaches/contacts is again emphasised

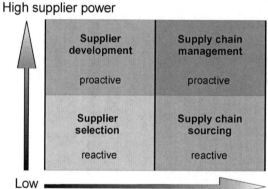

(After Cox et al of Logistics Europe June 2003)

A UK research survey, (After: Cox et al Logistics Europe June 2003), found the following breakdown in purchasing:

- 68% = Routine – commodity buying/supplier selection
- 12% = Bottleneck – reduce risk-preferred supplier/supplier development – collaboration?
- 13% = Leverage – reduce price-preferred supplier/supply chain

sourcing, collaboration?
- 7% = Critical – competitive advantage-partnerships/supply chain management, collaboration

Therefore varied sourcing approaches are found – it will however be noted that three of these involve collaboration. For the writer, the suggestion that supply chain management is only involved in one quadrant, as shown above, is not supported. Supply chain management as commonly used and as earlier defined, will also be involved in all of the above buyer/supplier dealings of supplier selection, development and supply chain sourcing. The approach of Cox et al is however a most valid one in showing that all purchases and relationships are not equal and in also showing where most of the transactions take place, (i.e. in routine commodity buying).

World class purchasing guidelines

- What are the annual spend and requirements of the purchasing portfolios?

- Is there a programme to reduce the procurement lead times?

- Is component variety limited by looking at users' specifications (avoiding brand names), and duplicated purchasing?

- What are the supplier assessment methods and supplier management policies?

- Do all communication processes deliver understanding?

- What codification is used?

- Is supply chain management used?

- Is end-to-end product evaluation used by applying the total costs of ownership (TCO)?

- What programme is there to develop relationships with users/ customers and with external suppliers?

- Is there a culture of Total Quality?

- Have buyers changed from being reactive order placers to being proactive commodity managers?

- Should you outsource or manage procurement yourself?

- Is there a programme to reduce the supplier base to a small number of qualified suppliers fully integrated into the business?

- Is there a culture of continuous improvement?

Production – 'make'

Production and manufacturing in the UK has been relatively late in changing to embrace demand-driven needs for smaller, make to order batches. The conflicts between volume and variety are a main aspect in production and traditionally, high volume with low variety (and low price), was seen as the 'only way'. However changes have been made in those industries that have remained in the UK. Meanwhile off-shoring has been the method used for much of the former UK manufacturing and production base.

Making to Order or Making to Stock
This is the separation point between forecasting and ordering and gives five 'positions' or 'decoupling points'.

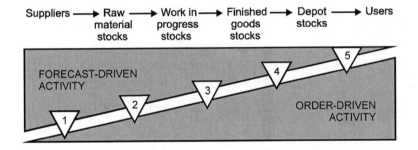

The 1-5 positions, separated by Forecasts and Order activities, are as follows:

1 **Make and deliver from stock** = Forecast driven. Examples are fast moving food products that are held in regional distribution centres, near to retail outlets.

2 **Make to stock** = Forecast driven. Examples are slower moving consumer and food items that are held more centrally in Central or European Distribution centres.

3 **Assemble to order** = Order driven. Furniture and beds are examples of this method of production.

4 **Make to order** = Order driven. Examples here are PCs and top of the range cars like a Rolls Royce

5 **Purchase and make to order** = Order driven. High-tech and large capital one-off items are examples here.

From a production aspect, the following can be found.

1 **typically continuous flow production** with very high volume produced but with no product variation; such as with petrol and steel. Such items are known as 'runners'

2 **typically dedicated line flow production** with very high volumes made and with little product variation; the mass production of cars was traditionally a good example.

3 **typically mixed product line** flow with medium volumes produced of medium product variations; the manufacturing of clothes is an example here as is the 'newer' method now used for car assembly. Such items are known as 'repeaters'

4 **typically batch flow production** with lower volumes of high product variation; job shops like printers being an example here.

5 **typically job shop production** of very low volumes but very high product variations, project one-off items like ships being one example. Such items may be called 'strangers' as they are not found too often!

These positions give rise to the following supply chain basic options where:

● 'Push' involves forecast-driven activity that pushes and supplies stock towards the customer, where it is held to await the customers demand orders. It involves the inventory holding of finished goods and is 'risky' in as much as it dealing more with uncertainty in demand.

● 'Pull' involves actual demand orders pulling stock through the supply chain from the point of supply. It is responsive directly to these orders and involves the products matching exactly what customers order. It involves the holding stock of semi finished work in progress, or even no inventory at all, (as with DP5), where raw materials are ordered to specifically manufacture a customer order. There is less risk with this option as nothing is more certain than the customers order.

Activity	MTS(1/2) 'Make-then-sell' Forecast 'Push' Supply-demand	MTO(4/5) 'Sell then make' Order 'Pull' Demand-supply
Main driver	Forecasts Structured planning and scheduling	Orders Sense and respond using real time information.
Buying	Is for anticipated needs by instructing suppliers Focus on cost and quality	Is for daily needs using involved suppliers Focus on speed, quality and flexibility
Product	Standardised products Cost driven	Can be bespoke and modular More quality driven
Customer lead time	Fast and short	Slower
Production	Low cost as uses long production run lengths High average utilisation	Higher costs and short run lengths and fast production line changes – excess buffer capacity is used
Inventory	Cost is in finished goods and uses safety stock Stock is viewed as an asset and as a protection	Cost is in raw materials and work in progress with little safety stock Stock is viewed as a liability

Distribution	Storage costs are high with low transport costs (as moving in bulk)	Storage costs are low with transport costs being higher as moving smaller quantities more frequently

The 'make then sell' position is well represented by the Henry Ford expression of 'you can have any colour you want, as long it as it is black', and by the traditional manufacture/assembly of consumer goods. However, nowadays for example, cars follow the 'assemble to order' (position three, above) that involves assembling a specific order from stocks of components/work in progress. This method of production represents for many, the optimum production trade-off in the supply chain as final assembly is only taking place on receipt of the order; the final product production being 'postponed' until a firm order is received. It also means adopting a more challenging form of supply chain management.

World class production guidelines

- Is product delivered on time in full (OTIF) more than 99% of the time?

- Is there a programme to reduce production lead times?

- Are materials received fit for purpose and supplied to the point of use without inspection?

- Do all communication processes deliver understanding?

- Does the layout enable sequential operations?

- Are set-up times reduced to the minimum?

- Is supply chain management used?

- Are non value added costs progressively reduced?

- Is there a culture of Total Quality?

- Is there an active policy to keep areas clean and tidy?

- Does the product design facilitate production?

- Is there a culture of continuous improvement?

- Should you outsource or manage production yourself?

Physical distribution – 'move'

Definitions

Definitions can be important to clarify thought and are especially so, when one person understands a term to mean one thing, but then another person understands the same term differently. This has been especially happening for example, in the UK from the mid 1990s with 'Logistics'.

Logistics, which originally encompassed the whole supply chain, is now being referred to by many companies as a new name for transport, or for warehousing/stores or for distribution. Third party transport companies are also now beginning to call themselves supply chain management companies. In the UK, one can observe the new name on a freight transport vehicle that before was called 'Fred Smith Transport,' is now called 'Fred Smith Logistics'. Logistics can therefore be a confusing word. Additionally, some people use the term logistics to describe there own internal company process, and use the supply chain term, when they are dealing with external suppliers/customers. At the risk of further confusion, others also call their internal logistics processes, their internal supply chain!

Physical Distribution, meanwhile, is about delivering the right goods to the right place at the right time and at the right cost. This 'rights of distribution' definition represents in a simple way, the objectives for distribution. Distribution therefore involves the combining of transport with warehousing, and is a term that is often applied to mainly finished goods. However, if may also by used by suppliers who are delivering product to their customer, perhaps of raw materials and semi-finished work-in -progress goods. Suppliers are also concerned with getting the 'rights' correct and as far as that supplier is concerned, the raw materials can be for them, the finished goods.

Supply chain management has been defined earlier. Meanwhile, when readers hear the three terms of *logistics, supply chain* and *distribution*, they are strongly recommended to ensure they have the full understanding of what the originator means by the specific word. This can be very important to prevent confusion. For example, 'Fred

Smith Logistics' is unlikely to have a clue about whether to outsource the manufacture of sub-assemblies or whether these can be manufactured internally. This would often be strategic supply chain decision, (but then again, some would say it is strategic logistics decision).

Distribution and the supply chain

Physical distribution is the method by which goods move from one location to another.

It is an essential function in product supply chains as it provides for the physical movement between the suppliers and customers. This movement can be for raw materials, sub-assemblies/work in progress, or for the finished goods; it can take place over shorter distances on a national basis, or the movement can be over longer distances and on a global basis.

In demand-driven supply chains, warehouses are mainly used for storing goods, or involve more sorting activities; both being required to largely feed external customers. In the supply-driven supply chains, warehouses often are re-named as stores, and are holding stocks to feed internal activities, like production. Transport and warehouses are both therefore, integral parts of the supply/demand chain/pipeline infrastructure.

World class distribution guidelines

The following are the basic points that everyone involved in managing distribution must be alert to.

- Do you need each warehouse in the distribution network?

- Is there programme to reduce all the distribution lead times?

- How can each item be packed?

- What products should be kept and where?

- Is product delivered on time in full (OTIF) more than 95% of the time?

- Is supply chain management used?

- How many times are products handled?

- Are products stored in relation to the flow/rate of movement?

- Is the warehouse layout and transport network optimal?

- Is the right transport mode being used?

- What are the operational standards?

- Do we have a multi skilled work force?

- Is there a culture of continuous improvement?

- Should we outsource or manage distribution our self?

- Is there a culture of total quality?

(All of this section on Distribution has been taken from the author's two books on the subject: *'Logistics Freight Transport – domestic and international'* and *'Warehouse Management'*. Readers who are interested in more detail on physical distribution may wish to refer to those books).

Marketing – 'sell'

It is customer demand that drives the 'total' supply chain; therefore the marketing process has some useful viewpoints. As has been usefully noted by Peter Drucker,

'Marketing is so basic that it cannot be considered a separate function. It is the whole business seen from the point of view of its final result, that is, for the customer's point of view ... Business success is not determined by the producer but by the customer.'

It is interesting to observe that marketing, like supply chain management, has gone thorough many changes in recent years:

Forward marketing 'Old'	Reverse Marketing 'New'
Production led as everyone would buy	Market led to determine what everyone needs to buy
Design and make the product first	Find out the customer needs and then design the product
High volume, low variety = 'Any colour you want as long as it is black,' (Henry Ford)	Customers needs are known in advance of production
Sell what you produce and promote unbought goods	Make only what you can sell and make to order
Focus on sellers' needs and make to stock	Customer satisfaction and loyalty

Basic tenets of marketing

- Customers are the basis of the business.
- We need to know who they are and what they need.
- We must anticipate customers changing needs.
- Everyone in the organisation is involved in marketing.
- We must develop long-term relationships with our customers.

(It will be observed that these tenets are the same for demand-led supply chain management).

The Marketing 'Ps'

A cornerstone of a marketing approach is the 'Ps'.

Product/service supplied looks at the following:
- Features (physical, service, psychological)
- What does it 'look like'?
- What will be delivered?
- Description, including benefits
- Value to the customer/WIIFM (what is in it for me)?
- Customisation/tailoring?

Place
- Distribution channels; how to get products to the marketplace, e.g. direct, via wholesalers, via retailers etc.
- Market positioning and competition in the marketplace
- Inventory levels; where and what format to hold?
- Physical distribution management; the moving of products to the marketplace
- Internet marketing and 'e' shopping

Physical facilities
- Premises
- Impacts to first time visitor/users
- Stationery/PR material/appearance

Price
- Cost plus process , or
- Market nature/market based prices?
- Competition pricing
- Customer perceptions and expectations

Promotion
- Communications
- Two way/understanding
- 'The object of communication is to prevent misunderstanding.'
- 'The meaning of communication is in its effect.'
- Moving through stages of unaware-aware-comprehension-conviction-action
- Using negotiation/persuasion

People
- Image
- Skills and experiences
- Attitude and behaviour

Working through the 'Ps' will show the basis of customer's needs and the resultant differentiation required and supply chain design.

World class marketing guidelines

- Who are the key customers?

- What differentiates the company from the competition?

- When was the last SWOT (Strengths/Weaknesses, Opportunities/Threats) analysis undertaken?

- When was the last PEST (Political, Economic, Social, and Technological) analysis undertaken

- Is the market place fully understood?

- Is there a culture of Total Quality?

- What is the market segmentation policy?

- Do customer contact staff have the authority to fully resolve problems?

- Do all communication processes deliver understanding?

- Is the 'time to market' at a minimum?

- Is there a flexible workforce?

- Is there a culture of continuous improvement?

- Is the company a market driven one?

- Is supply chain management used?

5

Supply Chain Strategy

The strategic aspects involve 'how we will win' and means having an awareness of the expected development of the business in terms of the future:

- product format, volumes and through-puts
- inventory holding
- suppliers and purchasing methods
- production method
- physical distribution method
- customers and marketing methods.

The strategic direction will be assisted by having a mission for the supply chain.

Mission-vision

From the forgoing discussion, it is possible to view that the mission of supply chain management is to have:

- transparent flows
- flexibility
- share to gain approach
- a reliance on quality
- elimination of all barriers to all the internal and external activities

- elimination of inventory whilst optimally balancing costs, service levels and availability.

Inventory

In the supply chain, then the flows of goods and information will need coordinating to minimise inventory levels. Inventory levels can often be viewed as the main 'poorly' symptom of a supply chain, and the root cause which therefore needs treatment.

Inventory is also the common component throughout the Supply Chain, either as raw material, sub assemblies/work in progress or as finished goods (which are often held at multiple places in the supply chain). It can also be the 'knock on' from one player to another player, as seen earlier in the Forrester effect (see page 43).

To prevent such effects, 'one number' views at individual SKU levels of the forecasts and orders are required through the supply chain. Inventory is therefore an important component to understand; also any changes in the supply chain structuring will inevitably have impacts on where and how much inventory is being held.

As Supply Chain Rule number two has already noted; the format of inventory and where it is held is of common interest to all supply chain players and must be to be jointly investigated and examined

Inventory management is an approach to managing the product flow in a supply chain, to achieve the required service level at an acceptable cost. Movement and product flow are key concepts as, when the flow stops, then cost will be added, (unless the stored product is one that appreciates in value over time).

Key aspects that are to be considered in inventory management are:

- determining the products to stock and the location where they are held
- maintaining the level of stock needed to satisfy the demand (by forecasting of demand)
- maintaining the supply
- determining when to order (the timing)
- determining how much to order (the quantity)

The supply chain is all about satisfying demand and this is found in two basic forms.

- **Independent or random demand** is independent of all other products; e.g. tyre manufacturer for puncture repairs. It is the classic consumer-driven demand for 'end use' products or services and therefore is more random, with uncertainty being found. It uses re-order point/level systems for inventory management/replenishment.

- **Dependant or predicative demand** is that derived from consumer demand which produces 'end use' products or services: e.g. tyre manufacturer for new cars, which is driven by the derived requirement for new cars and is planned for by the car assembler based on their view of the independent demand from consumers. With dependant demand, this means that the previous event has to happen first and that subsequent events will then depend on the ones preceding them. Dependant demand is therefore more certain for suppliers, enabling some degree of anticipation. For example, the tyre manufacturer obtains from the car assemblers their forward planning on production. It uses requirement/resource planning systems (MRP)

ABC analysis

A useful step is to analyse the products in terms of fast/slow movers by conducting an ABC Analysis exercise. This involves the classic Pareto analysis named after the 1890s Italian economist who reckoned that 80% of the wealth lay in the hands of 20% of the population. A high incidence in one set of variables equates to smaller incidence in a corresponding set of variables. The results of a product analysis will, classically, show that:

- **A items** – fast movers = high volume, few lines
- **B items** – medium movers = medium volume, medium lines
- **C items** – slow movers = low volume, many lines

If the ABC analysis is undertaken on a product value basis, then the following purchasing/stocking situation may apply in a manufacturing company.

- A items – high value items = low stock holding needing continuity in supply/JIT or periodic review (explained later). Bulk chemicals are examples here.
- B items – medium value items = minimum/maximum or continuous review system (see later) with supplier weekly check on stock/re-order. An example could be protective paints.
- C items – low value items = two bin system (see later) for such as nuts, washers

The following stocking policy is an example for in-bound supplies to serve production and is based on product values:

- A items are tightly controlled with orders only for known requirements. Continual accurate records/progressing with less than two weeks safety stock being held.
- B items are moderately controlled with ordering against forecast based on historic demand. Safety Stocks of 6-8 weeks were held.
- C items are at a lower control level with larger levels of safety stocks around 12 weeks

Why hold stock?

The following is a summary of the reasons why stock is held:

- **Decouples supply and demand**; stores and warehouses for example, actually 'sit' between supply and demand. Here the following examples of stock maybe found:
  - from the supply of raw materials to establish production
  - from work in progress and semi-assembled items, perhaps awaiting customising products
  - finished goods stock; for immediate demand order filling

- **Safety/protection**
  - to protect against supplier uncertainty
  - to cover for non forecasted demand
  - provided physically, by the warehouse

- **In anticipation of demand**
  - promotional or seasonal build up
  - bulk supply price discounts

- **To provide service to customers** (internal, external)
  - cycle stocks of finished goods
  - availability from safety stock for non forecasted demand

There may also be pipeline inventory in the supply chain. This would be stock in transit either from suppliers and/or to customers. The time in 'the pipeline/in transit' may be considerable if goods are undergoing a long sea journey.

In financial accounting, stock improves the company balance sheet. Stock is therefore an asset in financial terms. However, holding stock also carries costs (as we shall see later), which will appear in the financial profit and loss accounts. The turnover of inventory also means sales and profits to a trading business, therefore the faster the inventory turns, then the greater the profitability.

Inventory and uncertainty

A key aspect of inventory management is dealing with uncertainty, not only with the supply and the customer or consumer demand, but also in asking whether the uncertainty is 'real' (and is definitely caused by the dynamic aspects of the supply chain), or caused by institutionalised and out-dated/ill-informed procedures and lack of communication. Ann example of this is the Forrester Effect that can result when institutionalised demand distorts the real demand as it passes down a supply chain as each part views demand as being random. This can cause fluctuations and dependencies that can limit subsequent events occurring, as these depend on the last previous dependencies and are therefore being influenced by the fluctuations of the preceding dependencies.

Where the supply chain is long, with no end-to-end visibility, the length of dependencies in turn increase, meaning higher inventory carrying and slower movement as each dependency 'struggles' to undertake its activities due to the fluctuations. They 'struggle' with the capacity as the demand and the flow are not in balance.

Inventory costs

These are caused by many aspects. Consider for example the 'external' costs that accrue from any Forrester effects, and the cause of these costs that come from many different 'internal' activities and departments of a company. Many of the costs may be hidden from view. The following cost items can be involved:

Capital investments
- value of stock holding
- warehouse investment
- warehouse equipment investment
- ICT systems investments

Plus ... product holding costs
- storage/handling, (if not in above)
- obsolescence
- deterioration /damages to stock
- insurance

Plus ... ordering costs
- purchasing
- warehouse receiving
- finance payments

All these individual cost items equal the total cost of inventory, i.e.

Total cost of inventory = total of capital investment @ cost of borrowing money per annum
+ holding total costs per annum
+ ordering costs per annum
+ any other, specific, annual costs.

As an example, a large multinational oil company indicates the following percentage costs of its inventory value per annum:

Physical storage	3-5%
Deterioration /obsolescence	2%
Opportunity cost (cost of capital tied up)	12-23%
Total inventory costs	**17-30%**

Inventory service

This centres around the level needed (the availability), to satisfy demand. This will usually be a strategic decision of the business, but it also can be a decision taken at a lower level and one being taken to provide cover against complaints and 'noise' factors. Inventory is a dynamic and interactive process, so such 'anti-noise' low level decision making can be reflections that inventory it is not fully understood and that sub-optimal decision making is occurring in the business. The levels of stock being held to satisfy demand should be a company policy decision based upon an objective view of the requirements of users and customers. In a market situation, what the competition is offering will also have an input into the strategic decisions.

Inventory and lead time

Lead time has been looked at earlier. It is critical in making inventory decisions, as the following simple example illustrates:

- If use is 70 items per week, and supply LT is 2 weeks, then maximum stock is 140 items.

- But if the supply LT is variable by +/- one week then, the maximum stock is 210 items and the minimum stock is 70 items.

- But we may 'play it safe' and hold 210 items.

This is not the best decision but maybe an understandable one for those who are left to base replenishment decisions on protecting against personal 'noise' factors when past stock-outs have occurred. In such cases, then clearly inventory management is also not understood or involved both strategically and operationally in the business.

Inventory and statistics

Inventory management involves the manipulation of historic data by statistical analysis to give objective information on which decisions can be made. Statistics involve questions of probability that an event will happen, so with inventory management, statistics are a classic application for these techniques. Normal distribution is often used which describes the frequency of occurrences with some probability of an occurrence, which if graphed, follows a bell-shaped curve. It is defined by two parameters, the mean or average on the vertical axis and the standard deviation or the spread on the horizontal axis. Standard deviation is therefore used to describe the spread of the numbers and the difference from the average, or mean. In inventory management forecasting, the mean is the forecast demand, and the curve represents the forecast error. In inventory management for random demand and when calculating safety stock, the curve represents the service level factor. The following table shows the relationship between the standard deviation (SD) and the service level factor for availability of stock.

Service Level	SD Factor	Service Level	SD Factor
50.00%	0.00	90.00%	1.28
55.00%	0.13	91.00%	1.34
60.00%	0.25	92.00%	1.41
65.00%	0.39	93.00%	1.48
70.00%	0.52	94.00%	1.55
75.00%	0.67	95.00%	1.64
80.00%	0.84	96.00%	1.75
81.00%	0.88	97.00%	1.88
82.00%	0.92	98.00%	2.05
83.00%	0.95	99.00%	2.33
84.00%	0.99	99.50%	2.58
85.00%	1.04	99.60%	2.65

86.00%	1.08	99.70%	2.75
87.00%	1.13	99.80%	2.88
88.00%	1.17	99.90%	3.09
89.00%	1.23	99.99%	3.72

What is critical here is the effect on the level of safety stock required to satisfy random demand. For example, note the increase from 95 to 98% (plus 3%) means a 25% increase in the standard deviation/the extra stock to be carried.

Increasing service levels gives an exponential curve relationship in the extra safety stock required, as the relationship is not a straight line; for example, a 3% increase in stock does not equal a 3% increase in the extra stock required. It will also be seen that there is a huge increase of 226.8 % when moving from 95% to towards the mythical 100% (or 99.99% in statistics, as there is always the probability).

Higher service levels for stock availability with random demand mean proportionately far higher levels of stock are carried. The subjective 100 per cent availability that is commonly stated as a requirement is a myth for random demand. This needs to be known about by all people in a company and the varied levels to be objectively accessed.

Of course, the idea of setting, say, a 90% service level for stock availability is fraught with problems for customers and for sales/marketing. All they rightly expect is 100% service and levels below this mean little to them. The key aspect here is that customers will always get their demand requirements satisfied, for example by back ordering, and how we deal with the other 10% will influence how the level is set in the first place, what the extra costs are for maintaining higher levels of stock and also how the supply chain is operated. With the acceptance of back-ordering, this will often provide an acceptable service for non-stocks with a firm date for delivery.

In many companies, the majority of profit will also come from a relatively small number of lines; the 80/20 rule again. So here safety stock levels can be set to minimise the value that may be on back order and minimises the cost to the company. Lost sales are however extremely difficult to analyse and some companies see it is better to let a competitor have such sales to prevent the high cost of stocking relatively slow moving low profit lines.

How much stock should be held?
Looking at this simply, then there are three basic aspects to be considered here:

1 **If decoupling supply/deman**d, then we need enough to cover for the difference between the input and output rates. This is called bulk or quantity (Q) stock and is the inventory to be used for routine demand consumption. If we have constant demand and supply lead times, then the following is the position:

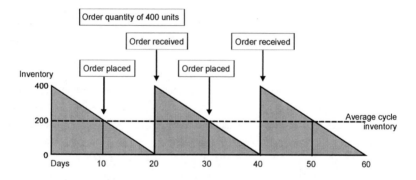

The re-order level (ROL) is fixed here at a quantity of 200 and the re-order point (ROP) is fixed at a time period of 10 days; the level being dictated by the demand and supply lead times.

2 **If uncertainty with supply,** then we need to have cover for the expected use during the supplier lead time. This is called safety stock (SS) and is held to cover the supply.

3 **If uncertainty with demand,** then we need enough to provide availability until the next delivery. This is also called *safety stock*, held to cover the demand.

When we have uncertainty with demand or with lead time then safety stocks are carried, as illustrated by the following:

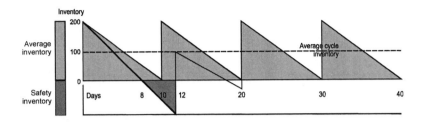

Any one or all of the above three situations may be involved. This also illustrates the two types of stock that are found:

- **Cycle stock** (or replenishment or lot size stocks). These are held as a result of in and out movements and involve decisions on order quantity and frequency

- **Safety stock** (or buffer or fluctuation stocks). These are held as a 'cushion' between supply and demand (either or for both) and involve decisions on supply lead time (SLT), supply lead time variability (SLTV) and the amount of demand that will occur during the SLT/SLTV.

It should be appreciated that these two types of stock are not held separately, but are only separated out in the calculation for the 'when and how much to order' stock decisions, as we shall see later. Some people do use the words 'working stock' for the cycle and the safety stock together.

Another way to think about stock is with the analogy of a car fuel gauge. When the tank is full, then we do worry about supply. When it falls to 50%, we may then start to think about when we need to get some petrol (the 'how much to order and when' inventory decisions). We may wait to do this until the warning light flashes which causes us to think: 'Where can I get a supply of petrol and how much will I be using before I can get a new supply?' This illustrates the need to plan when to order. Whilst we can always wait until we run out of petrol, this is not really best practice as it will incur time penalties, extra cost, inconvenience etc.

When we properly plan when to order, we will consider the options of:

- a variable time, for example, whenever we might pass a filling station or when the warning light flashes (VOT)
- a fixed time, as we will plan to go to the filling station, say every Friday (FOT).

When we then get to a filling station, and assuming they have stock available, we have then to decide how much to order. The options here are as follows:

- fill to top, therefore we get variable order quantity each time we order (VOQ), or we
- fill with say £10 worth, therefore we place a fixed order quantity (FOQ).

This analogy introduces us to the reality that the 'when and how much to order' decisions can have a fixed or variable time to order with a fixed or variable order quantity. The following shows the possibilities, with some 'realities'.

Option	Meaning	Comments
FOQ/FOT	£10 every Friday	May run out before the FOT, but acceptable if constant demand and lead times, as in the basic EOQ method.
FOQ/VOT	£10 when passing a filling station, or, after the warning light has flashed	Needs a more continual review of stock
FOT/VOQ	Check every Friday and then fill up the tank if needed of stock	Needs a periodic review of stock at the fixed order time interval (e.g. Friday)
VOT/VOQ	Fill up when passing a filling station or, after the warning light has flashed	Too many orders are being placed and virtually a full tank is being maintained

The above introduces us to the main inventory replenishment methods of continuous review (FOQ/VOT) and periodic review (FOT/VOQ). There are some other variations on these two: minimum – maximum and two-bin methods for inventory replenishment and these will all be looked at shortly.

Replenishment methods

Before considering further the how much and when to order decisions it will be recalled that demand is found in two basic forms:

- **Independent or random demand**; this is independent of all other products; e.g. tyre manufacturer for puncture repairs. It is end consumer driven and random, and therefore has more uncertainty and uses re-order point/level systems for inventory management.

- **Dependant or predictive demand**; this is due to demand elsewhere; e.g. tyre manufacturer for new cars (OE). It is more driven by the derived demand of supplier/customer ordering, enabling more anticipation, and more certainty than is found with end product consumer buying. Dependant demand uses requirement/resource planning systems (MRP/MRPII).

We will now examine each of these two different types of demand and the methods used for replenishment.

Replenishment for independent demand – the 'when to order' decision

This will be simply; 'when stocks at a level that is able to satisfy demand, until the replenishment order is available' This in turn requires the following questions to be asked.

- How much demand is expected during the supply lead time?
- How long will replenishment (the supply lead time) take?

There are two methods that can be used to check to see if an order should be placed:

- **At a specific time period (ROP).** This is called periodic review but it is also called the *periodic inventory time based method*, the *order up to level system* and the *fixed order interval method*. This has a fixed order time period (FOT), e.g. weekly at the 'trigger' of the time.

- **At a specified level of stock remaining (ROL).** This is called *continuous review* and is also called the *perpetual inventory action level method* and the *fixed order quantity method*. This has a variable order time period (VOT), e.g. when at the ROL of the 'trigger' of the quantity in stock

When making replenishment decisions, then the following will need considering:

- **Supply LT (SLT)** is the time that follows from determining the need, deciding to place an order, up to the time it is available for issue. Accuracy of data is needed and the SLT includes many different steps involved, as shown by the earlier lead time explanation. SLT therefore includes the external suppliers lead times, plus the internal steps of the requiring/ordering between customer/user and the receiving/available for issue lead times. It is surprising that many companies do not know objectively what their SLT's are. This simply means therefore they are not effectively controlling their inventory

- **Supply LT Variability (SLTV)** if applicable. This is also usually poorly dealt with; SLT must be measured on a continual basis to identify any variability.

- **Average demand (Av.D)**, or the forecasted demand, during the supply lead time. This is sometimes called the lead time demand, which more correctly is the demand during the supply lead time.

- **Demand variability (DV)**, if applicable. This is the difference between the average demand and the actual demand, over time and it is measured by the standard deviation.

- **Setting a required service level (S/L)**, to ensure the correct stock level is held and is available to service requirements to cover against any supply and or demand uncertainty.

Where demand and supply lead times are certain, predictable and known, then the calculations are easier; known and fixed supply lead times with known and fixed demand create far simpler decisions. For example:

Fixed demand   50 units per week
Supply LT   2 weeks
Then one order option is 100 units ordered every two weeks.

The keys to having such predictability are found for example where:

- historic demand and supply lead time are good proxies for the future

- long mature product life cycles – no promotional product activity.

However for most companies, such certainty is not the real world and conditions of uncertainty are normal. For example, the marketplace works against certainty with demand volatility and increased product variety by introducing new products and competition. Reduced and shorter product life cycles limit the value of historic data and additionally, wider global supply bases cause complications for supply lead times. All of these changes to demand and supply lead times mean greater safety stocks are required.

The following will illustrate the calculations to cover against the 'probability' that we will be dealing with uncertainty:

1.0   Average demand   50 units per week
        SLT   2 weeks
        Demand variability   12 units
        Service level   95% (1.64 standard deviations)

2.0.   Then 50 x 2   =   100 (cycle stock)
         $12 \times 1.64 \sqrt{2}$ =   28 (safety stock)
                       ROL   128

So the overall formula is:

    Av.D x SLT; for the cycle stock/demand lead time, plus
    DV x S/L $\sqrt{}$ SLT; for the safety stock:

3.0.   To illustrate the concept of variability again, if we get SLT variability of 1 week, then:
    50 x 3   =   150 (100 cycle + 50 safety stock)
    $12 \times 1.64 \sqrt{3}$ =   34 (safety stock)
                    ROL   184
    Here the 'extra' for the variability is 50 + 34

Some important conclusions are possible from this example:

- The longer the lead-time, the more safety stock.
- LTV is critical.

Replenishment for independent demand – the 'how much to order' decision

From our earlier example of filling a car with petrol, we saw that the options were as follows:

- fill with say £10 worth – therefore we place a fixed order quantity (FOQ), or
- fill to top – therefore we get variable order quantity each time we order (VOQ).

Looking first at the fixed/constant order quantity (FOQ)/continuous review-variable order time (VOT) interval options first, we can identify several points.

- Each time there is an issue/withdrawal from stock, the stock position is reviewed to see if a replenishment order is needed.

- The same quantity is ordered each time, but it is ordered and delivered at varied times, e.g. 10 tonnes week 1, 3, 4. Suppliers are therefore expected to deliver when needed with any quantity required.

- The quantity to be ordered uses the economic order quantity (EOQ), less the free stock. EOQ finds the optimum order quantity, at the balance between the cost of placing and the cost of holding, an order. (Both EOQ and free Stock are explained below).

- The decision on whether to order is triggered by the ROL. The ROL is calculated from the demand lead time (Average of demand x Supply lead time), plus the safety stock calculation (DV x S/L $\sqrt{}$ SLT)

With the Variable order quantity (VOQ) /period review-fixed/constant order cycle time (FOT) interval, other points arise.

87

- The stock position is reviewed at a fixed time to see if a replenishment order is needed. As this is at a fixed time, this can then facilitate more regular deliveries from suppliers.

- A variable quantity (VOQ) for each order is placed at the same time, e.g. 1, 3, 5 tonnes ordered every Friday to 'top up' back to the targeted maximum inventory level required.

- The time period (FOT) setting is influenced by EOQ, (for example, annual demand quantity divided by the EOQ gives the number of orders per annum) with the high annual usage items being ordered more frequently.

- The maximum level for more stable demand and SLT can be determined by the EOQ. For more uncertain demand/SLT, the maximum level is determined by the average of demand * supply lead time, plus the safety stock (DV x S/L $\sqrt{}$ SLT), plus, an additional allowance of average demand x review period, (for demand before the next review period).

- The quantity ordered (VOQ), the 'up to level,' is the maximum stock level, less the free stock.

There are some other simplified variations for inventory replenishment with independent demand – the two-bin and the minimum – maximum methods.

The **two-bin method** is a simple form of the continuous review method that starts with the holding of two identical quantities of maximum stock, the maximum stock being that needed to cover the supply lead time. One 'bin' lot is then used to satisfy demand and when this bin is empty (the ROP); the second bin is then used and an order placed to replenish the empty bin. The order quantity is therefore fixed at one bin (FOQ) and is placed at a variable time (VOT) as the usage will vary before reaching the ROP/ROL. The two-bin method is useful for low cost, high demand items that have large order quantities. So if a new order has a SLT of two weeks and the usage is 10 items per day per full week, then 140 items is the ROL and ROP.

Minimum-maximum is a method that has a maximum level set, for example, set at the EOQ plus the ROL. The minimum level becomes the ROL and this is set by the average demand, the supply lead time and safety stock. When the ROL is reached (at a VOT), then orders are placed at the required quantity to return back to the maximum level, therefore giving a variable order quantity (VOQ). Similar to the basic EOQ model, min-max has more varied order amounts. It is analogous to the thermostat on a heating system – when the temperature gets below the minimum, then the boiler is turned on and supplies heat at a rate dependant on how much the temperature has fallen, and how much heat is being consumed during the lead time required to restore the room temperature to the required level.

Economic order quantity (EOQ)

This is a simple way to determine the order quantity and the size of an order. It is found at the balance between the cost of placing and the cost of holding, an order. EOQ makes assumptions that there will be no stock outs, zero lead times and that we can 'safely' order when at zero stocks. This is really not realistic when faced with uncertain demand, the need for variable order quantities and supply lead times with variability. However, where repetitive ordering occurs, EOQ should be considered, for example, make to order, purchase for stock holding (such as wholesalers) and stable maintenance, repair and overhaul (MRO) items.

As essentially an accounting formula, EOQ requires much data, which may not be readily available, such as the holding and order costs, the different line items, the demand and the product unit costs.

EOQ will not therefore apply in every situation. It does however give indications for re-order levels and points; it also emphasises the importance of calculating order costs.

EOQ Model

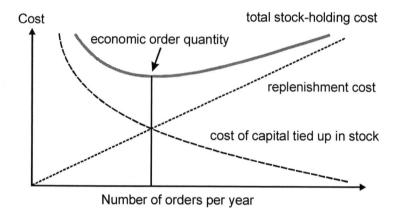

The order (or inventory or cost of capital tied up) costs fall with the number of orders, whereas the holding (or carrying or replenishment) costs rise with the number or orders.

The formula is as follows:

$$EOQ = \sqrt{\frac{2 \times R \times S}{C \times I}}$$

R = Annual demand   say 3000
S = Order Cost   say £20
C = Product Unit Cost   say £12
I = Holding Cost   say 25% of C

$$EOQ = \sqrt{\frac{2 \times 3000 \times 20}{12 \times 0.25}} \qquad = 200 \text{ units}$$

The above figures used are for illustration only as each company will need to verify its own figures. Benchmark figures in literature can be dangerous. For example, on order costs, the writer has seen quoted figures of £5-£15 at the lower end and £50-£75 at the higher end – quite a variation for alleged standard benchmark figures!

Exaggerated costs are the common mistakes when using EOQ,

whereas in reality small variations will generally have little effect. Critical costs must however be always calculated by each company and be re-evaluated at least once a year. The critical costs are the order cost and the holding cost, and these are considered below.

Order costs

It may not always be appropriate, for example, to include all the costs incurred in purchasing/ordering and warehousing/holding, as shown below. For the **order costs**, if repetitive and regular ordering is undertaken, then the fixed order costs are lower than a long tendering process for one-off items when, for example, capital equipment is involved. For purchasing externally, then the order costs would include the cost to enter orders, any procurement process approvals and also processing after receipt, such as quality checking, invoice checking and payment. With internal ordering, such as requisitions from stores, then the order costs represents the time to make the work order, time with selection/picking/issuing and the inspections.

To calculate the order costs, it can be more effective to determine the percentage of time spent performing the specific activities and multiply this by the total labour costs for a time period, typically a month, and then dividing this by the units processed in this time period.

Order costs are mainly therefore the cost of people in processing orders, but it may also include communication costs.

Holding or carrying costs

This represents the cost of having inventory on hand; such as the storage costs and the investment costs. The investment cost is calculated as the value x interest rate and the insurance charge (which is related to the value of inventory).

The storage costs are frequently mistaken, as these should be the variable costs based on storing stock/inventory and not on all the fixed and variable costs of running the warehouse. The deciding factor is, are the costs directly affected by the inventory levels? If yes, then include the costs.

The cost per pallet stored is useful here, but then care is still needed as average values can be misleading as one pallet could contain £100,000 or £100 value of product. As the costs are applied in the formula as a percentage of the inventory value, then inventory needs to be classified based on the ratio of the storage space to the value. For example, the pallets of high valued product are allowed for separately from the pallets of low valued products.

Meanwhile, the conclusion from purely an EOQ point of view is to order the high annually used items often, and the low annual used items are ordered more infrequently. When being used to determine a specific order quantity, EOQ is useful for minor stock items of low values with known steady prices, demands and supply lead times. Where there is demand variability, such as seasonality, EOQ can still be calculated but using shorter time periods; ensuring that the usages and holding/carrying costs are also based on the same time period. EOQ is not really appropriate where there is random erratic demand with price fluctuations and variable supply lead times.

Comparisons: continuous and periodic review

The following comparison between the continuous and periodic review replenishments methods illustrates the main differences:

Parameter	Continuous Review FOQ-VOT	Periodic Review VOQ-FOT
How much to order, plus, need to allow for the Free Stock position: The stock on hand, plus any stock expected less any stock allocated or being kept for special use.	A fixed order quantity (FOQ) when at the ROL. Typically the EOQ is ordered.	A variable order quantity (VOQ) , (as dependant upon what has been used since the last fixed time check and what is now needed, if any, to bring back to the 'up to level'). Allow for Av.D x SLT, plus Av.D x Review Period, plus the Safety Stock calculation.

Parameter	Continuous Review FOQ-VOT	Periodic Review VOQ-FOT
When to order	When at the ROL therefore a variable order time (VOT). The ROL is calculated by the Av.D x SLT plus, the Safety Stock calculation	Fixed order cycle (FOT), as there is a predetermined time when to order. The time is influenced by the EOQ (annual demand quantity, divided by the EOQ, giving the number of orders per annum)
EOQ	Amount to order when at ROP	Helps in setting the review period frequency
Assumes/Prefers	Certainty with constant demand, lead times and prices throughout a period. Suppliers have to deliver at any time.	Can deal better with uncertainty. Suppliers can make regular deliveries
Stable demand	Lower safety stocks	Higher safety stocks as protecting over a longer time period
Seasonal/variable demand	Higher stocks due to big demand swings	Lower stocks
Control	Needs continual/perpetual monitoring of inventory levels, therefore is more responsive	Checked at the review period only
Usage	Most common for low value items and infrequently ordered 'C' items. Used by industrial manufacturers.	Most common for high valued and critical 'A' items. Used by FMCG industry as gives a rhythm for checking whether to place and order or not.

Comparisons: Managing inventory by value and volume

High Value	Low Volume	Medium Volume	High Volume
	1 for 1, poisson distribution	PR: 7 to 14 days	PR: 1 to 7 days with fixed lead times
	Average periods forecasts	Exponential smoothing forecasts with seasonal, trend and error tracking	Exponential smoothing forecasts with seasonal, trend and error tracking
	Parameters reviewed every 3/6 months	Parameters by tracking signals reviewed 4 times per year	Parameters by tracking signals reviewed monthly
Medium Value	CR	CR: Q on EOQ, ROP on av D + SS	PR: 14 to 28 days
	Average demand forecasts, plan for seasonality	Average demand forecasts	Exponential smoothing forecasts with seasonal, trend and error tracking
	Parameters reviewed every 3/6 months	Parameters reviewed every 1/3 months	Parameters by tracking signals reviewed 1/3 months
Low Value	Two-bin	CR: Q on 6-8 orders p.a. ROP on av. D + SS	CR: Q on EOQ, ROP on av D + SS
	Average demand forecasts	Average demand forecasts	Average demand forecasts
	Parameters reviewed every 6/9 months	Parameters reviewed every 1/3 months	Parameters reviewed every 1/3 months

Replenishment for dependant demand – materials planning (MRP/MRPII)

It will be recalled that this is due to demand elsewhere, e.g. a tyre manufacturer for supplying tyres to new cars (original equipment, OE). This is a more direct customer-driven decision which enables more anticipation and more certainty. It uses materials requirement planning systems (MRP) which are integrated computer systems planning tools used in production/manufacturing that determine the following.

- What input materials are required?
- How many?
- When needed?

Also used is manufacturing resource planning (MRPII) and follows on from MRP but adds in production capacity calculations. MRP is also one the parts of ERP (enterprise resource planning) systems such as SAP.

The basics of an MRP system are shown below:

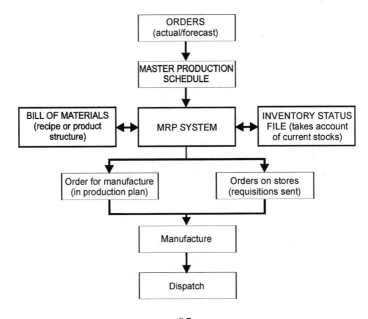

MRP has the following basic principles:

- Demand information goes into the master production schedule (MPS) which covers a specific time period and allocates the demand for each product into time buckets of days or weeks.
- The component structure for each product is held in the bills of materials file (BOM) which is the menu of parts and sub-assemblies item by item.
- MRP calculates from the top level of the BOM the gross requirements needed. It then accounts for quantities in stock or already on order and then calculates the net requirements for the item. If there are any batching needs, such as a minimum order of 100 items, these are allowed for and finally the MRP logic calculates against the lead times for supply and brings forward order dates accordingly. It then goes on to the next level of items until the lowest level of the BOM is reached.
- The output from MRP is a set of time phased materials requirements showing how much and when each item should be purchased.

To be effective, MRP needs accurate forecasting and well defined product structures in the bills of materials files (BOM), along with known and reliable supply lead times.

A common error however in some MRP applications is the reality of unreliable supply lead times and also, the default original lead time settings may have never been reviewed to reflect changes. In theory, MRP systems will give the stores known and predictable receiving times for stocks that should only be held for a short time; indeed cross-docking activities should follow MRP applications.

Replenishment, free stock and current stock balance

The above discussion has considered when an order point trigger can be calculated. Of course it is more than likely that stock is on hand and this must therefore be allowed for.

The current stock balance will be recorded that allows for issues, receipts, orders placed etc. What is needed however is the measurement against the order point trigger, the so called 'Free Stock' position. This is an adjustment to the current balance that allows for any of the following conditions:

- addition of stock already ordered
- addition of stock in transit (if not recorded in the stock already ordered)
- subtraction of stock already allocated to customers from the current stock balance
- subtraction of stock on hand being retained for any special purposes.

Seven Rules for Inventory

1. All inventories should be justified, and, minimised, with the target being zero inventory.

2. Staff needs training and motivating to correctly identify, locate and count all inventory correctly.

3. Safety stock should only be held to protect variable demand to give customer service, or against variable supply.

4. Orders should only be placed when a stock-out is anticipated.

5. Re-order just enough to cover demand, until the next receipt is due.

6. Focus effort on the few important items and not on the trivial many.

7. ICT can help and take away the 'number crunching', but manual checks and reviews are still needed.

Finally, in this look at inventory, the following summary will illustrate how inventory can be planned.

Model for planning inventory

1. **Establish whether current performance is cost or service driven?**

2. **Conduct an ABC analysis and demand analysis**
    e.g. focus on the important few not the trivial many

3. **Consider reducing order quantity options**
    e.g. reorder only enough to cover demand until next receipt
    e.g. increase order frequency consistent with EOQ

4. **Measure and consider reducing safety stock**
    e.g. hold only when protects service against variable demand
    e.g. SLT and SLTV
    e.g. check service levels are needed
    e.g. reviews
    e.g. measure and improve forecast accuracy
    e.g. reduce number of stockholding locations

5. **Reduce finished goods stocks**
    e.g. move towards make/assemble to order
    e.g. reduce variations, obsoletes, low sale items
    e.g. make smaller batches

6. **Review and check parameters manually and regularly, the target being zero inventories**
    e.g. Analysis at item level
    e.g. order more frequently at item level

7. **Aim for short fixed lead times with accurate demand forecasting**

Supply Chain
Key Performance Indicators (KPI's)

Supply chain performance will be driven by the following:

- **Organisational configuration of the physical assets and product/information flows** – for example, elimination of inventory whilst optimally balancing costs, service levels and availability
- **Management of the supply chain** – for example, flexibility and a reliance on quality
- **External relationships with suppliers and customers** – for example, a share to gain approach
- **Internal structures and management of the supply chain** – for example, elimination of all barriers to all the internal and external activities
- **Information systems** – for example, transparent flows of goods/information

The entire supply chain performance can be measured by the following measurement tools:

Description	Measurement tool	Definition	Units
Customer orders fulfilment	On time/in Full rate (OTIF)	% orders OTIF	%
	Lead time	Receipt of order to despatched/ delivered	Hours/Days
Customer satisfaction	Customer Survey	A sampling survey to ask for custom-ers' experiences, for example: -Support available -Product availability -Flexibility	% satisfied

		-Reliability -Consistency -Comparison to the competition	
Supply management	On time/in full (OTIF) Supplier Survey	As above As above customer survey	% satisfied %
	Effectiveness.	Year over year improvements	%
	Lead Time	Time placed order- time available for use	Hours/Days
Inventory (measure for each holding place of raw materials, work in progress and finished goods)	Forecast accuracy	Actual/Forecast sales per SKU	%
	Availability	Ordered/Delivered Per SKU	%
	On hand	Value on hand/ daily delivered value	Days
Cash flow	Cash to cash	Time from paying suppliers, to time paid by customers	Days
Quality	Quality	Non conformances, as appropriate	Per 100 or 1000 or million
Operations	Utilisations Productivity Costs	Used/Available Actual/Standard Actual/Standard.	Units Hours Costs
	Lead times	Time start/time completed per operation, (see the earlier Lead time section)	Hours or Days

People Relationships	Internal	Absence rates Staff turnover rates	% %
	Internal	Opinion surveys, for example: - Support given - Development - Morale - Work conditions - Communication - etc	% satisfied
	External	Sampling Survey, as used in the above customer surveys	% satisfied
Costs	Total supply chain or per operation cost.	Cost per time period/units	£ per unit

Supply chain metrics and strategies

No single strategy will ever sustain in the long run due to the ever changing dynamic market and external demands. Supply chain strategies will need to be constantly worked on. The following diagram shows one way to monitor the strategy.

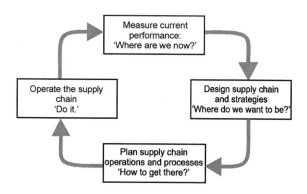

To assist in monitoring the supply chain further, the following questions may help:

1. When were all of the lead times last examined?
2. When were all of the supply chain processes mapped?
3. Were value-added and non-value-added activities clearly identified?
4. What barriers are there to increasing service and reducing costs?
5. Are there multi-functional teams working on improving materials and information flow?
6. Have manufacturing and supply lead times been reduced in the last three years?
7. Have lot sizes and set-up times been reduced in the last three years?
8. Have all inventories been reduced in the last three years?
9. Are inventory buffers in existence to protect against quality problems?
10. Are there agreements with suppliers and mutually agreed goals for continuous improvement?
11. Are suppliers certified to 'no inspection' required?

12. Are communications 'fit for purpose' and are both electronic and also face/face?
13. Is lead time precisely known for replenishment and for customer deliveries?
14. Is little time spent on expediting?
15. Are performance measures weighted towards short lead times and quick response with minimal inventory levels?

Supply chain analysis

For those who may have been 'stirred' to examine their supply chains further, then the following may be used to examine the current supply chain network.

1. Describe the current supply chain process that exists, between your suppliers and your customers. Cover all the applicable lead times from the users need order placement, to being finally available for issue/use by, customers/consumers.

2. Describe each of the activities, in the current supply and order fulfilments processes. For each activity, (for example, pre-order planning, procurement, suppliers, transit, receiving, warehouse, transit, receivers), provide the following information:

   - Activity decision
   - Frequency that activity occurs
   - Who is responsible for that activity
   - Information required to conduct that activity
   - Average activity lead time
   - Minimum activity lead time
   - Maximum activity lead time
   - Cause of activity lead time variability
   - Activity KPIs
   - Activity current KPIs

3. What KPIs do you use to assess the overall supply chain performance in your company?

4. What impact do the current processes have on your company?
5. For the inventory, describe the types/format (RM/WIP/Finished goods) and amounts (value/quantities/days of supply) that are held in your company.
6. Why is this inventory held?
7. As for item (5), what are the inventory levels being held downstream by suppliers and upstream by customers?
8. Why is this inventory held?
9. What actions could you take to improve the lead times for supply?
10. What actions could you take to improve the lead times for customers?
11. What actions could your suppliers take to improve the lead times for supply?
12. What actions could customers take to improve the lead times for customers?
13. How far downstream and how far upstream the supply chain do you need to extend your analysis?
14. What are your suggestions to make this actions happen?

Supply chain trends

Following this analysis, then the following trends may give some 'directions'.

Customer demand decisions

● Define what drives customer service, then develop and design the 'on-demand' supply chain against market needs; it is demand that 'kick starts' the whole process.
● Understand the supply chain requirement for customer segments (and tailor as appropriate).

Product decisions

● Products will vary – for example, standard, segmented standard, customised standard, tailored customised, pure customised.
● Design products for interchange ability, ease of assembly, and standardised parts.
● Assemble to order, customised products.

- Postpone final product differentiation until the product is required.

Strategic decisions

- Need a top commitment to the supply chain purpose/vision that recognises that it is fundamental to integrate independent processes for interdependency.
- Leverage e-business to link assets and process, across partners.
- Minimise fixed costs, keeping assets and resources flexible.
- As supply chains are collections of business that add value, then focus on the core value drivers and then perform more added value work.
- Outsource non-strategic and non-competitive activity, (DIY or Buy In).
- Adopt and enforce common performance and quality standards throughout the supply chain.
- Use flow logistics by designing all processes for the continuous flow of goods and information, therefore minimising lead times and stockholding.
- Design and manage adaptable supply chain networks.
- Manage through a cross-functional organisation and structure.
- Appreciate flexible relationships across the supply chain.
- Continually develop the people, so that they will continuously improve.
- Concentrate on the five key aspects and the eight supply chain rules areas.
- Remember that supply chains may appear to be technically simple, but remain managerially difficult.

6

Supply Chain Thinking and Approaches

With supply chain management being a dynamic and changing philosophy, then new and varied approaches develop. Sometimes these are merely old practices that have been slightly changed and dressed up with a new 'sexy' name; sometimes these represent good and inventive thinking. We shall look briefly at some of the latter.

Quality management

Whilst certainly not a new approach, Quality Management is very supportive and a valid approach for Supply Chain Management. Quality management represents the involvement and commitment of everyone, in continuously improving work processes, to satisfy the requirements and expectations of all internal and external customers. It is therefore somewhat fundamental to Supply Chain management; as will be further seen in its **ten basic principles**.

- Agree customer requirements.
- Understand and improve customer/supplier chains.
- Do the right things.
- Do things right first time.
- Measure for success.
- Continuous improvement is the goal.
- Management must lead.

- Training is essential.
- Communicate more effectively.
- Recognise successful involvements.

There are several options available to use:

Kaizan means continuous improvement in a gradual and ordered way. It has an objective of the elimination of waste in the processes, components and functions. It has two parts: one being improvements and change and the other being to do this ongoing and continually.

Total Quality Management is an approach towards larger scale company change and improves existing process and functions. TQM needs strong direction and leading from the top as it needs commitment and involvement from all. As such middle management in traditional command and control structures can often be a barrier to TQM, as the managers fear a loss of control as their jobs become largely superfluous as involvement spreads 'below' them.

Six Sigma involves statistics, as in the use of sigma (or the standard deviation), to establish company benchmarks which assist in work processes being continually improved to meet the customers' expectations. It has a 'goal' that the chance of failure is only 3.4 in a million opportunities. Whilst this may be unattainable, it does indicate that six sigma, like Quality generally, represents often a 'journey to a destination'. The six key concepts are:

- **Critical quality**: what actually is it that matters to the customer?
- **Defects**: what happens when fail to deliver what the customer wants?
- **Process capability**: what the processes can do.
- **Variation**: what is the customer's perception and how does this differ from the critical quality?

- **Stable operations**: what has to be done to ensure consistent and certain processes?
- **Design for six sigma**: what is involved in designing to meet customer needs and to get process capability?

Reverse Logistics

This may be defined as 'the management of returns from users back to senders', 'the management of returns from stores back to the store for resale, to the supplier, to consumers through appropriate channels or for disposal' or 'closing the supply-chain loop by recapturing the value'.

The process: collection – return to designated site – checking condition – collation – recovery/disposition – redistribution.

Key areas

- The technology/ information to say 'why' they are to be returned; are they faulty, are they damaged, are they not needed (for example: clothing catalogue goods returns = 18 to 35%, electrical catalogue returns = 4 to 5%).
- The sender's scanning and tagging, if any.
- The process of coming back, the 'how' (for example: collection by delivery vehicles, assessment, categorising).
- The feedback and performance information (for example: to buyers or marketing). Life cycle product costing approaches of cradle to grave are emphasised here.
- The assessment on receipt and the disposition options (see below), and the space required to do this (do offsite?)
- The returns policy of the companies involved, for example: the supplier and the retailers policy may vary.
- The full financial implications of the process

Recovery and disposition options for reverse logistics

Inspection is needed by 'expert eyes'. The basic options are:

1. No change to the original state = re-use of overstocks, excess inventory.

2. Dismantling to re-use = recovery/re-manufacture or refurbishment.
3. Extracting of elements to be used as raw material elsewhere = repair/reconditioning of damaged products; replacement of missing components, recovery of packaging and product.
4. Return to supplier; perhaps for disassembly into parts for recycling
5. Disposal to landfill sites

These options then may involve re-stocking, resale, scrapping obsolete products or parts. Consider in all, the legal implications and environmental restrictions

Collaborative supply chains

Supply Chain rule number three observed that the optimum and the 'ideal' in Supply Chain Management will only ever be found by *working and collaborating fully with all*. As we earlier noted, the change from transactional methods to collaborative approaches goes far beyond the technical issues, of say ICT connectivity, and fully embraces the soft skills. Supply chain management collaboration between companies, where appropriate and when required, will not succeed without appropriate recognition that soft skill development is required. This section will examine, albeit briefly, this largely soft skill area.

The barriers to collaboration can be viewed as followed:

Barriers	Comments
No trust	Fear here is usually of giving information to competition
Poor communications	Usually meaning there is no up to date sharing and also a comment on the format of communication being used
No 'big picture' view	Too focused on 'own' issues and problems

No risk taking	Fear of having 'all eggs in one basket' and a preference for 'playing off'
Prefer a power-based adversary transactional approach	Annual contracts and three quotes, common the public sector continue to perpetuate adversary approaches in procurement
Want quick and short term wins	In reality success will depend on time and effort over longer periods
No sharing of benefits	The power view of 'keeping it all' whereas all should save from mutual collaborations.
No planning, all 'kick and rush'	Collaboration is hard work involving soft skills. It also will need adequate planning
No support for any changing 'how we do things'	Top support is important
'Output is king and anyway we are too busy fire-fighting'	Concentration here is on the 'operations' and looking just for short term efficiency whilst ignoring longer term effectiveness.
Fear of change	Remaining with the 'status quo' in times of change/stable turbulence is akin to the ostrich analogy of burying the head in the sand.
Fear of failure from the existing blame culture	Change to a 'gain' culture.

The benefits of collaboration in the supply chain have been noted as follows:

Aspect	Collaboration brings
Forecast accuracy	Increased external visibility forces better accuracy
Lead time	Reductions following sharing and joint improvements

Inventory	Reduced as stock levels fall
Utilisation of resources	Improved in a 'leaner' operation with less waste
Costs	Reduced and improved
Service levels	Increased and improved
People	Trust and improved relationships

Rules of collaboration

These are that real and recognised benefits must be found for all internal and external players. This will involve:

- business process integration at all stages
- support collaboration of all the supply chain components
- recognition of the culture
- the importance of people relationships – and when improving relationships, it is useful to remember that:
  'It is the soft stuff that is the hard stuff.'
  'People may be physically present, but are they there psychologically?'
  'Only when all people come together is found the power of one.'

What fundamentally therefore has to be changed?

People first … and also …

- contracts to simple flexible approaches
- intensive management involvement
- periodic performance monitoring
- internal controls for confidential information
- problem solving procedures
- supplier is seen as a customer = 'reverse customer service'
- cross-functional supplier/customer teams
- hub (supply chain managers) and spoke (suppliers/customer) organisations?

And people last … as 'people change one at a time'.

It is people that change a company and it is the people who make the relationships in and between companies. The process of changing company culture ('what is done around here') will need to pass through the following stages:

Aspect	'Stormy/Blame'	'Steady/Sane'	'Sunny/Gain'
Goals	Announced	Communicated	Agreed
Information	Status symbol and power based	Traded	Abundant
Motivation	Manipulative	Focused on staff needs	A clear goal
Decisions	From above	Partly delegated	Staff take them
Mistakes	Are only made by staff	Responsibility is taken	Are allowed as learning lessons
Conflicts	Are unwelcome and 'put down'	Are mastered	Source of innovation
Control	From above	Partly delegated	Fully delegated
Management Style	Authoritarian/ aggressive	Cooperative	Participative/ assertive
Authority	Requires obedience	Requires cooperation	Requires collaboration
Manager	Absolute ruler and feels superior	Problem solver and decision maker	Change strategist and self confident

Once the culture has been defined, this will need the examination of all internal and external relationships. Trust will often remain a major barrier; but, without trust, there is no relationship.

Trust is fundamentally about 'having to give up to another what you personally believe is valuable to you.' It is 'One for all and all for one' and it is a 'willing interdependence.' Trust is firstly built between people, one on one, and is not something that is built remotely between nebulous companies. The following are therefore involved when building trust 'one on one':

- doing what you say you will do
- going beyond conventional expectations
- undertaking open and honest communicating
- being patient
- accepting and admitting to mistakes
- ensuring the other party gets a fair outcome.

Collaboration therefore is basically sharing together and involves:

- **shared goals** = common purpose, collective commitment, and agreeing the business we are in
- **shared culture** = agreed values that bind us together, working cooperatively to the common goal
- **shared learning** = pooling talent, skills, knowledge, reflecting, reviewing, revising and changing together
- **shared effort** = one approach with flexible teams
- **shared information** = the right information is shared with the right people for the right reasons, where the:
  - **right information** = that which is used to give better service and reduce costs
  - **right people** = are those who can use it to help you
  - **right reasons** = that which will 'reduce, save, improve, quicker' etc. (Source after: Partnerships with People)

The 'how to get there' is not going to be easy. The following section on 're-thinking' tells us why this may be.

Supply chain re-thinking

Many people do now understand what is involved when following a supply chain approach. However, ensuring the supply chain is optimised for the benefits of all participants will mean a re-thinking of traditional ways.

Such re-thinking may not be an easy process for some individuals in some companies and this may therefore limit the optimum development of supply chains. It would seem a possibility that Supply Chain development in the UK may well falter because of the prevalent way of management thinking.

What however is sure, is that what worked for many years, may not work for many more.

Supply chain development

Supply chains can be at various stages of development and the following gives a view of possible developments:

Stage	Structure of the supply chain	Some actions needed
'Starting out'	Fragmented and uncoordinated. Low cost/ service levels, high stock levels	Internal alignments. Coordinate external suppliers Measure supply chain efficiency
'Getting there'	Some working together but still high stock levels	Supply chain structure ICT systems internal/ external for transparency/visibility
'Arrived?'	Has a supply chain structure but have slow growth and competition increasing	Develop new sales channels Modular products Direct delivery to customers Integrate fully the ICT systems
'Re-birth'	Static market growth	Increase out sourcing. Strengthen existing relationships, Branding, R&D, marketing
'Starting out again'	Virtual structures	Active monitoring and remain flexible for the 'next' changes

Changes when using a Supply Chain approach

The supply chain approach will require changes to 'the way we do thing around here'. The following briefly illustrates some of the needed changes

Changes	Some of the needed 'ends' are:
'Silo' functions to 'holistic' processes	Decision integration, organisations of extended enterprises, collaborative management approaches, web connected, real time focus
Product 'sells' to customer 'buys'	Demand pull, order driven, low to zero stock holding, involved suppliers, short production runs, real time visibility, short product life cycles, fewer suppliers, market segmentation
Transactions to relationships	Dependency , commitment, cooperation, collaboration, aligned company cultures, extensive trust, proactive management

The way we look

A Supply Chain approach will therefore require a business to change and this, in turn, will mean changing the thinking from a current and known position, towards a possibly unknown but planned-for future. As the way we think affects what we do, then the way we think, is an important process to be considered.

Research suggests our brain is in two parts – the left hemisphere and the right hemisphere. At least, this is the simple view – front and back, upper and lower quadrants are other 'divisions'. Indeed, research into brain activity continues to contribute to our understanding at a rapid pace.

Meanwhile, the left and right view suggests we have a **logical left-side brain** and a **creative right-side brain**. The left-side brain will firstly conduct an *analysis*, will then *act*, and finally will *feel*, (for example, is the action 'correct' and 'right'). The right-side brain however, works the other way, *feeling*, then *action*, then *analysis*. Most people are relatively flexible in this brain wiring and of course the influences of environmental forces and the way we are nurtured,

115

treated, handled etc also has a powerful impact to our thinking and to our personal behaviour. In exploring simply, the left side-right side brain differences, then the following is revealed:

Logical left-brain sided people	Creative right-brain sided people
Prefer written, mathematical, science-based approaches	Prefer musical, art/visual-based approaches
Objective, linear thinking, short-term views	Subjective, wholes/parallel processing longer-term views
Analytical, step-by-step 'head' thinkers	Creative, free-flowing 'heart' thinkers
Rational, facts-based reasoning that converges	Emotional 'feelings' synthesis that diverges
Summary: Analyses-acts-feels	Summary: Feels-acts-analyses

Most individuals can usefully recognise which side is their personally representative one.

The way companies manage

As companies are collections of individuals; it is therefore possible to see left-side and right-side companies. Following on from the above individual brain-sided view, companies may be viewed as follows:

Left-brain sided companies	Right-brain sided companies
Task based 'today.'	People based and a long term view.
Problems reoccur as only the symptoms are treated ('Elastoplast' solutions)	Problems are tackled by looking at the thinking that causes the problems.
Making/selling products-services has the priority	Make people before products-services

The way forward is with science/ technology	The way forward is by motivating/ empowering people
'The numbers speak for themselves'	'It is how we connect together that is important'
Incremental results/parts.	Holistic, whole results/parts
More Western cultural based	More Eastern and Latin cultural based

Left-sided companies will often work with fixed assumptions for development and growth as they are incapable of 'thinking outside the box'. When they are pushed to change from their 'tradition', they will react negatively as they fundamentally believe the way forward is 'more of the same' and they see the only solution to, for example, company growth, is needing a bigger share of the existing market.

Supply Chain thinking

The ways of thinking will also translate into company management approaches, including how supply chains are managed and structured, for 'as a person thinks then so they are' (Proverbs 23.7).

The following diagrams represent a thought process for the past and future of Supply Chain management.

1. Older approach/linear thinking

This model has given proven benefits to the previous non-supply chain ways of functional silo management.

It will be seen that this approach represents linear thinking, which is classically left-brain mode. This approach is also the major model

117

currently used in the UK for supply chain development. By following the above left-brain explanations, we can see that this means having short-term, task-centred approaches with an incremental view of the supply chain, with relationships to the next level only. This may or may not involve a collaborative approach and will more than likely have fixed arrangements and contracts in place. It will tend to use a rigid and reactive approach to customer service with scheduled and rational replenishment.

The supplier may also feel that the supply chain coordinations are all one way and that 'coercive power' is being used; this being noted for example as 'the bullying and exploitation in which supermarkets indulge' (L. Michaels, March 2004).

2 Newer approach, network thinking

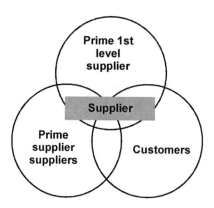

Here there is some attempt to go further into the supply chain using collaborative approaches and extending beyond the first supplier level. Fixed arrangements with boundaries/contracts may exist but the collaboration will be more open and sharing. Customer service can be more responsive and flexible with real time replenishments.

3 Emerging approach/systems thinking

In this model, much more fluid arrangements occur, with systems thinking recognising the complex interactions that affect each other player in the specific supply chain. Right-brain thinking concentrates on the wholes of the supply chain and perhaps uses seamless collaboration and virtual arrangements. Collaboration will be totally open and shared, and is unbound and innovative.

Each specific supply chain could be viewed as a small company in itself, comprising cross-internal functions and jointly managed with suppliers/customers, maybe following a matrix/project management structure organised into specific supply chain cells with decentralised control and shared responsibility from all involved. This follows the basic principles of 'small within big' that has, for example, worked successfully when adopting TQM and JIT methods for production cells internally within product manufacturing/assembly organisations. Interestingly, such approaches were pioneered in Japan – a more natural right-brain culture – but of course, have been actively adopted and managed in the UK culture. Some changing in thinking went on.

A summary of the three models on supply chain thinking follows:

119

Old Supply Chain approach	Newer Supply Chain approach	Emerging Supply Chain approach
Linear thinking	Network thinking	Systems 'links and loops' thinking
Maybe collaborative at first level only	Collaborative and maybe beyond first levels	Collaborative and seamless in scope
Fixed contractual arrangements at 'arms length'	Fixed arrangements/ boundaries/contracts	Virtual arrangements, unbound and innovative
Horizontal flow chart	Venn shape	Petal/shamrock shape
'Rigid'	'Connected'	'Fluid'

Changing how we think

There have been many well known examples of former company sector leaders who have slipped from the number one position and also examples of former state-owned monopoly companies that no longer exist. Companies can therefore be slow to change their thinking. In Supply Chain management, the consequence of 'sticking to the knitting' thinking can be as follows:

- adversary play offs with suppliers
- long production runs of not-needed products
- 'just in case' expensive stock holding
- customers get fed up and go elsewhere
- inspection, reworking, warranty claims
- vertical silo management structures
- 'turf conscious' reactive 'fire fighting' managers
- 'rowing the boat' upstream and resisting change.

Companies are collections of individuals and it is the thinking of the individuals in companies that needs to change. As has been noted above, individuals will tend to be more 'happy' in one or other of the brain sides. This then means they can miss out on the other side. To be complete, we therefore need both sides. This is classic whole-brain thinking. Clearly many companies do try to reflect such whole-brain thinking through their recruitment policies and in the way they structure the organisation of the business.

But for efficient and effective supply chain management, companies and the individuals in companies need to take more conscious responsibility for the thinking. Business channels change and when taking the view that supply chains now compete, this can mean thinking in a different way. Those individuals/companies who do not do this, may well find that they will not be 'invited to the party' in the future. An example here is where a supply chain approach acknowledges that supplier numbers will be reduced; yet, some suppliers will maintain a head-in-the-sand, ostrich incremental approach, perhaps believing the reductions could not possibly affect them.

Thinking differently

Our brain is actually very similar to everyone else's, but the difference comes from how we use it. Individuals and companies should be challenged to use the brain differently.

If they are more on the creative right side, then the need is to be more of a logical left. The following could be tried:

As Individuals	For Companies
Be on time for appointments.	Keep promises and commitments
Practice and plan a step/step approach	Get the parts and processes working well, together
Time plan each step	Use time based KPI's
Have a work space that is ordered and structured	Reorganise the flows in the supply chain supply chain

If more of a 'logical left' side, then the need is to be more of a creative right. The following could be tried:-

121

As Individuals	For Companies
Brainstorm to create ideas.	Look at the whole supply chain beyond first level suppliers
Make visual mind map notes to enable free flowing visual images	Make a supply chain map of the business and its supply chains
Explore a new neighbourhood.	Explore how to get the people relationships 'right'
Try and understand your pet's feelings.	Try to understand how the staff 'feel'

The future: the right- or the left-sided company?

The optimum and the whole will only of course be found by using parts from all sides of the brain. The concern however is that remaining with traditionally British left-side thinking will very likely mean that the trends and ways forward for supply chain management are never realised. This can mean, for example missing a future of:

- a few long term suppliers and joint action teams in the whole supply chain
- short production runs with quick changeovers
- minimal stockholding, JIT type supply through the supply chain
- being able to serve more demanding customers
- obtaining right first time quality throughout the supply chain
- having process and flatter cross functional management structures
- empowered proactive fire lighting managers
- continuous improvement and change.

The way of thinking and the way the supply chain is structured and managed are therefore critical. The reported benefits of following a supply chain approach have been usefully documented; it will be noted that different approaches give significantly different results:

	No supply chain: functional silos	Internal integrated supply chain	Plus, external integration to the first level only
Inventory days of supply Indexed	100	78	62
Inventory carrying cost % sales	3.2%	2.1%	1.5%
On time in Full deliveries	80%	91%	95%
Profit % Sales	8%	11%	14%

It will be seen that by following a supply chain approach, then the inventory costs fall, profit and service fulfillment increases; the 'best of both worlds' for the company undertaking the approach. This is why supply chain approaches have been actively pursued by those companies looking for lower costs and improved service levels. It is very clear therefore that supply chain management works.

What is also especially interesting here is that the structure of the supply chain is shown. Furthermore, the network thinking supply chain that goes beyond first level suppliers and the systems thinking one, should both indicate savings beyond those of the supply chains that stop at first level integration.

But many companies will choose consciously to remain with the power based 'winner takes all' supply chain approaches of the adversarial pursuit of 'value for me alone', and will remain content with dealing at the first level only. This clearly may be appropriate and be seen as good business when the measure of success remains with profit for me alone. However in a future of market-driven forces and increased uncertainty, one wonders how long companies having old established structures and holding such one-sided views will survive, without re-structuring internally and without having to find new strengths externally beyond themselves.

Releasing the strengths of collaboration and cooperation externally will arguably only happen when such players will also get a benefit. Thinking differently and looking for more creative and innovative ways to manage the supply chain may therefore be a future only a few companies are able to undertake. For example, moving to more collaborative approaches involves win/win and involves trust; this remains a most difficult aspect for those left-sided rational thinking companies who prefer to use the German word for partnership – *partnershaft*.

It would seem a possibility that Supply Chain development in the UK may well falter because of the prevalent way of management thinking. I am reminded of a Welsh saying that says; 'adversity comes with learning in its hand'. It could be painful to wait for the adversity and the associated hard lessons of learning from mistakes. One thing is very sure; what worked for many years may not work for many more. Therefore there is a real challenge to learn anew and in so doing, to change. Learning and changing are indelibly connected; you cannot have one without the other.

The 10 signs of World class supply chain management

At the end of this book on supply chain management, it is useful to reflect and revise on the key aspects. Whilst the eight supply chain rules and five key aspects, given earlier, do provide a useful overview of what supply chain management is essentially all about, the '10 signs' listed opposite bring together aspects that must be found in any 'world class' supply chain.

World class supply chain management

- It must be linked to and part of the corporate strategy.

- It must be seen as giving added value and competitive advantage to the business.

- Cross functional organisational structures must be found.

- Information must 'lubricate' all the processes and the decision taking.

- Key areas and performance are measured.

- Lead times are checked, reviewed and evaluated, regularly.

- Underpinning all decisions is 'customer first' and 'customer satisfaction'.

- A continuous improvement culture enables people development and fosters good relationships.

- External suppliers as viewed as being 'integral partners' with collaboration also found 'at home'.

- Trade-off analysis is undertaken.

Sources:

Anderson & Lilliecreutz, *The Change in Supply Chain Innovation*. 2003

Bell S, Letter in *Management Today*. March 2004

Best Factory Awards. 2001.

Cheltenham Tutorial College

Cox et al: *Logistics Europe*. June 2002

Emmett S, *Improving Learning for Individuals and Companies*. 2002

Emmett S, *Getting the people right in ILT Focus*. April 2003

Emmett S, *Logistics Freight Transport*. upcoming in 2005

Emmett S, *Warehouse Management*. 2005

Michaels L, Letter in *Management Today*. March 2004

Partnerships with People. Department of Trade & Industry. 1997

Porter M, *Gaining Competitive Advantage*. 1985 '

Signals of Performance: The Performance Measurement Group Volume 4. Number 2-2003